THE A-Z OF CURIOUS
SUSSEX

STRANGE STORIES OF MYSTERIES, CRIMES AND ECCENTRICS

WENDY HUGHES

The History Press

*For my friends at Worthy Words Workshops, Sea Scribes,
and a special thanks to Lyn McInroy, for all their
encouragement and support.*

First published 2017
Reprinted 2019

The History Press
The Mill, Brimscombe Port
Stroud, Gloucestershire, GL5 2QG
www.thehistorypress.co.uk

British Library Cataloguing in Publication Data.
A catalogue record for this book is available from the British Library.

ISBN 978 0 7509 5604 8

Typesetting and origination by The History Press
Printed in Great Britain

Contents

Introduction

The physicist, Albert Einstein said, 'The important thing is not to stop questioning. Curiosity has its own reason for existing. One cannot help but be in awe when he contemplates the mysteries of eternity, of life, of the marvellous structure of reality. It is enough if one tries merely to comprehend a little of this mystery every day.' This is certainly true when you look at the county of Sussex, defined by its spectacular walks along the chalky Southdowns and the dramatic rugged coastline. It is also the home of the infamous smuggling gangs, who would stop at nothing to bring their illicit cargo safely ashore. But behind this amazing façade, there is an assortment of tales of mystery, the strange, the extraordinary, the funny, the unexplained, as well as the bizarre and sad. Add to this the exploits of the 'stand and deliver' highwaymen, the shipwrecks, and with both Horsham and Lewis gaols in the county we have a fair share of gory crimes too.

The county also has its larger-than-life characters, its wacky inventors, its trailblazers who made their mark in society, which all add up to a rich collection of anecdotes. In this book I have attempted to seek out a few stories that are well-known and worth retelling as well as filling in the gaps of some lesser stories, and hopefully adding a few that are new and will allow the reader to understand a little about life's mysteries and never to stop asking questions.

I have tried to be informative and I hope I will be forgiven for choosing those versions of the stories that have appealed to me personally, the tales that made me question why a building was built or to seek out the curious story behind why something happened. As they say, you can't please everyone all the time, but I hope that each reader will discover between these pages something new and of interest to enjoy.

Wendy Hughes, 2017

⁂ ALBOURNE ⁂

∾ *Inventor extraordinaire* ∾

To start our voyage around intriguing Sussex we'll pick up a traditional mode of transport and take ourselves to the story of one of the most successful inventors of bicycles, tricycles and the differential gear, as well as the perfector of the bicycle chain drive. James Starley was born in 1830 into a farming family, who lived at Woodbine Cottage in Albourne. He was educated locally, and even at the age of 9 demonstrated an inventive mind by making a rat trap from a ripped umbrella and a branch of a willow tree. This enabled a duck to waddle through a hole in a fence, allowing the mechanism to close behind, so a rat or any other predator couldn't follow. Young James certainly didn't inherit the family flair for farming and at the age of 15 left home, walking via Little Horsted to Tunbridge Wells through

Woodbine Cottage, family home of James Starley (Conrad Hughes)

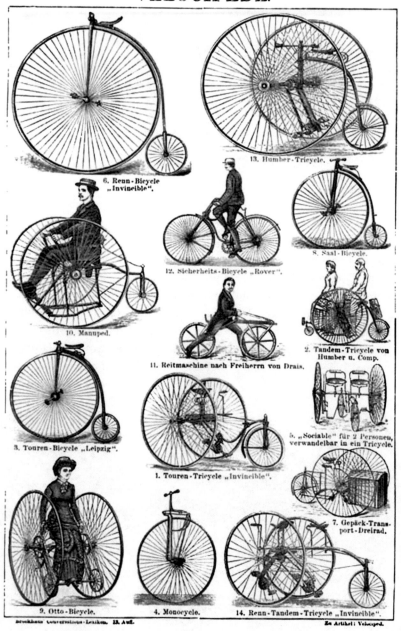

Poster showing the velocipede in various stages of development

Sevenoaks, to end up five years later at Lewisham where he obtained work as an under-gardener. In his spare time he mended watches and made useful items such as an adjustable candlestick and a mechanical bassinet to soothe the crying baby of his employer John Penn. John bought a rare and expensive sewing machine for his wife from his friend Josiah Turner, a partner in Newton, Wilson & Company, but it broke down, and he turned to James for help. He not only mended it, but improved the mechanism. John was so impressed that he rushed off to tell Turner, and James joined the factory in Holborn. Two years later in Coventry, Turner and Starley set up the Coventry Sewing Machine Company with James working on his own invention called 'The European', but his inventive skills were destined for bigger things. In 1868 Turner's nephew brought a new French bone-shaker called a velocipede to the factory, and immediately James could see room for improvement, and set to work on a version with a lighter wheel. Grabbing the opportunity, the company started making bicycles and soon became the centre of the British bicycle industry, especially with the *Ariel*, an all metal vehicle with wire-spoked wheels. By 1876 he'd developed the Coventry Lever Tricycle, using two small wheels on the right side and a larger drive wheel on the left, the power being supplied by hand levers. This was followed by the Coventry Rotary, one of the first rotary chain-drive tricycles, and a favourite with those who didn't feel confident on a high wheeler. Local folklore informs us that on a visit home, James sold one of his penny-farthing bicycles to Queen Victoria, after he overtook her horse-drawn carriage by sheer pedal power. After his death in 1881 James's sons continued to manufacture cycles, but it was his nephew, John Kemp Starley, and a colleague who made a difference by devising the modern Rover safety bicycle with 26in wheels. Even today the word Rover means bicycle in countries such as Poland. Of course the motor-driven bicycle gave way to motorcycles, followed by the motor car, and to think this may not have happened if James Starley had chosen a rural life amongst the corn and wheat.

⇻ ALDWICK ⇺

∾ *The stench of cooking fish* ∾

On a wet blustery December night in 1912 a young lady answered a knock on the door at Goodman House, home of Mr New. She was alarmed to find a soaking wet man, clearly distressed, speaking in a foreign language, with agitated hand gestures. The police were called, and an inspector and constable set out to solve the mystery. As they walked along Steyne Street they came across three bare-footed men covered in sand, and again despite the language difficulties established that their ship, *Carnot*, had beached. Meanwhile the local postman came across three men who indicated through hand gestures that their shipmates had headed off in the direction of Bognor Regis. Soon the crew were reunited, but no-one could understand them until Mr

New remembered Louis Peacock. He could speak French, and eventually their story emerged. It was now 11.30 p.m. on 29 December, and the policeman called George Walters, the local secretary of the Shipwrecked Mariners' Aid Society, took the men to the Pier Restaurant in Waterloo Square where they were given hot food before being settled for the night. A telegram was sent to Captain Bailbed's home in St Malo confirming that he and his crew were safe and well. The ship's dog, a large black retriever, was placed in the stables at Mr Peacock's home, but frightened, it howled until Mr Peacock took it inside where, exhausted from its ordeal, it went to sleep lying across Mr Peacock's chest. By now *Carnot* rested high up on the beach, its sails still raised. The coastguards, receiving a message about a vessel aground, sent the coxswain and a member of the lifeboat crew to investigate. When they arrived they found resident Mrs Croxton-Johnson looking at the ship in disbelief, and realising the lifeboat was not needed they returned to base. The following morning the Receiver of Wrecks arrived, and the coastguards took possession of the ship and cargo. Spectators from Bognor Regis gathered in the wintry sunshine to take photographs, and on Monday the *Carnot*'s hatches were opened. She had been carrying a cargo of 160 tons of cement and 110 barrels of herrings, and as the seawater mixed with the cement, it heated, the herrings baked, and the air was filled with the acrid smell of cooked fish, which the spectators said gave the impression that the ship was on fire. Meanwhile the crew were enjoying the hospitality of the town, with Mr Peacock acting as interpreter. Sets of clothing were quickly found for all, and Mrs Croxton-Johnson invited the crew to her home for tea. In the evening

The French crew with the grounded *Carnot* in the background (West Sussex County Library)

they were taken to a picture show at the Pier Theatre where a collection raised £2, and other donations amounted to another £2 4*s* (£2.20). The following evening they were taken to the local Kursaal theatre to enjoy a Christmas pantomime, *Babes in the Woods*. By now members of the French Consulate had arrived from Newhaven and took charge, arranging the purchase of new clothes for all at a shop in West Street, but when they returned to St Malo on New Year's Day, their captain and owner stayed, and was joined by his wife for an unexpected New Year break. I expect the smell of cooking fish became a talking point for many months to come.

⚜ ALFRISTON ⚜

∞ *Where did he burn those cakes?* ∞

The story of King Alfred famously burning the cakes is well known, but no-one knows exactly where it occurred. Some say it happened on the site of the Star Inn when it was no more than just a peasant's hut. Alfred was the Saxon king of Wessex when the Danes were busy seizing land from the Saxons, and after one particular battle Alfred found himself cut off from his soldiers. Alone, he was forced to flee, and legend claims that the hungry and tired king sought food and shelter in the hut of a poor peasant woman, who fed him and let him stay. After two or three days the king was well enough to think about how to regroup his soldiers and attack the savage Danes. Could he drive them from his kingdom for good? As he

Is this the village where Alfred the Great burnt the cakes? (Conrad Hughes)

was thinking about his next course of action, the woman asked him to watch some griddle cakes while she went about her daily work. Lost in thought the king soon forgot about his task and let the cakes burn. When the peasant woman returned and saw the burnt cakes on the hearth she scolded the king, and hit him with a stick. From this experience Alfred learnt of the need to always be vigilant. Is this tale true or not? Who knows? It is claimed that Alfriston means 'Alfred's town' and Alfred is known to have connections in the area. There was a royal palace at nearby West Dean, which he is supposed to have owned or used, so was he trying to get there when he became so exhausted that he had to stop?

∽ *Smuggling days* ∽

The Star Inn is believed to have been built as a hostel by the Abbot of Battle in 1345 to accommodate monks travelling to the shrine of St Richard in the city of Chichester. In the 1500s it was turned into an inn with numerous fascinating colourful wooden figures built into the front of the building. One is said to be St Michael fighting a dragon, and another is a bishop, perhaps St Richard? Outside the inn sits a rather strange-looking figurehead of a red lion, taken from a Dutch ship wrecked in Cuckmere Haven 300 years ago, and ransacked by the infamous Alfriston Gang. The leader was Stanton Collins, who came from a good family who lived at the Market Cross Inn, now the Smugglers Inn. When he took it over from his father he turned it into a bar and smugglers' haunt. It is a curious building with twenty-one rooms, forty-eight doors, six staircases and numerous hidden exits including tunnels, one of which led under the floor of the bar down towards the river, though that was filled in a while ago. If customs men came into the bar the smugglers could escape through a space beside the chimney into a secluded

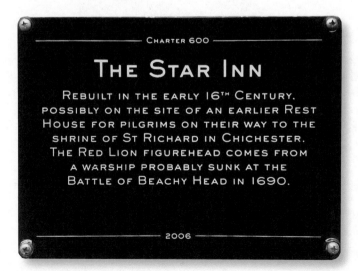

Site of hostel built
by the Abbots of
Battle (Conrad
Hughes)

The Star Inn as it is today
(Conrad Hughes)

The Smugglers Inn, home of
notorious smuggler Stanton
Collins (Conrad Hughes)

hideout, and when the customs men left, their friends would shout up the chimney that it was safe. The notoriously violent gang used the river (now a stream) that meandered beyond the High Street to bring their illegal gains from Cuckmere Haven to the village for distribution. The gang were never caught, but broke up when Stanton Collins was arrested, not for smuggling, but for burning a barn. He was tried at the Winter Assizes in December 1831 and sentenced to transportation to Tasmania for seven years, aboard the *Lord William Bentinck*. The gang had a reputation for being ruthless, and one tale tells us that one of the smugglers was in hiding above the cliffs overlooking Cuckmere Haven one dark night, waiting for a sign that the booty had landed. His job was then to alert the gang that it was safe to collect it. He was about to go and tell them when he noticed a revenue officer at the cliff top picking his way through the dark, guided by large chalk rocks set at intervals along the path. Of course the gang was well prepared, and had moved some of the rocks so they led directly to the cliff edge. As the officer tumbled down the cliff he yelled out, but managed to grab the edge of the cliff. The smugglers rushed from their hidey-hole, and stood looking down at the officer hanging on by his fingertips. He begged them to save him but one of the gang stepped forward and stamped on his fingers, sending him spiralling to his death. Everyone thought the officer accidentally fell in the dark and it was only a deathbed confession by one of the gang that revealed the truth.

∞ *Man's best friend* ∞

Towards the end of the 1700s the son and heir of the Chowne family of Place House Estate went for a walk with his dog, possibly a little white terrier. It was Midsummer's Eve, and as he walked along White Way, between Alfriston and Seaford, he was attacked near Dean's Place and killed by a blow to the head. He was quickly buried by the thieves in the roadside bank with his dog. Seven years later, a couple were walking along the road, and saw a small white dog disappear into the bank of the road, and on every seventh year after on the anniversary of the murder, the phantom dog, sometimes seen with his master, returned and disappeared into the bank. Then in the early 1800s when the road was being widened, the skeleton of a young man was discovered. His bones were removed and laid to rest in the church and the ghostly dog never appeared again, presumably content to know that at last his master was at rest.

⋇ ARUNDEL ⋇

∞ *A fright of ghosts* ∞

Most castles have a ghost or two lurking within their corridors, and Arundel Castle is no exception. Some claim it's the home of at least seven! First on the list and the oldest is the ghost of Earl Roger de Montgomery, 1st Earl of Arundel, who built the castle, and still keeps a watchful gaze on it from the keep, watching everything that passes by. But one of the saddest ghostly inhabitants must be the spirit of a boy who is thought to have worked in the kitchens 200 years ago or more. It is believed that his master beat him, and one day he struck him so severely that the poor boy died. His ghost has been heard, but not seen, on many occasions, scurrying around the kitchen, or feverishly scrubbing the pots and pans. The second saddest must be the ghost of a young lady who also used to work at the castle. She fell in love with a bishop but was rejected. Unable to cope, she killed herself by jumping off the top of Hiorne's Tower. She is seen, usually in moonlight, dressed in white and always crying as she wanders around the top of the tower looking for him. Strangest of all is the apparition of a man who frequents the library. No-one knows who he is, but he's wearing blue silk garments of Charles II period and has acquired the name of 'Blue Man'. Custodians have seen him searching through or reading the

Hiorne's Tower, allegedly haunted by the figure of a White Lady (Conrad Hughes)

books, although the book itself varies. He only stays for a minute or two before disappearing, so perhaps he is searching for some lost fact, an inventory or a will? Some say a cavalier haunts the library, but as there is very little known about him it has been suggested that it is just the Blue Man. The library is also the residence of a little black dog, belonging to Sir Philip Howard, 13th Earl of Arundel in the days of the reign of Elizabeth I. This earl was sentenced to death for failing to renounce his Roman Catholic faith, and although the sentence was never carried out, he spent eleven years in the Tower of London accompanied by his dog. Several of the guides have been asked, always by children, who does the little dog in the library belong to? As yet no adult has reported seeing it, so does it only appear to children? Finally, an alarming subject for a ghost is that of a small white bird, very similar in size and shape to an owl, seen on many occasions fluttering around the windows of the castle, but always just before the death of a resident. We do know that before the keep was restored the dukes kept a colony of white American owls. Is it one of them, I wonder? The most recent sighting of a ghost was by a trainee footman in 1958 who was on his way to switch off the drawbridge lights. Halfway along he noticed someone about 15ft in front of him going in the same direction. As he got nearer he could only see the head and shoulders of a man wearing a light grey tunic with loose sleeves. He had longish hair and he guessed the man was in his early twenties. The footman said the image was like an old photograph with the outline blurred, but he could see nothing below the waist. As he walked on the apparition faded and disappeared completely. The terrified footman ran back along the drawbridge forgetting to switch off the lights.

∾ Saints above, nuns, priest and an eerie tale! ∾

It is not known when the first church of St Nicholas was built, but the Domesday Survey records a church dedicated to St Nicholas between the years 1042 and 1066. The church is unique, being the home of two denominations, Roman Catholic and Church of England. In 1836, the Fitzalan Chapel was exchanged for land on which to build the new town, and in 1874 a brick wall was built next to the grille to divide the church, which resulted in a legal argument involving the Roman Catholic Duke of Norfolk, and the then Church of England rector, Rev. G. Arbuthnot, as well as a some nuns who'd been allowed to use it. The high court

Fitzalan Chapel was used as a barracks during the English Civil War (Conrad Hughes)

ruled that the chapel belonged to the Duke of Norfolk and so began the curious situation of two churches of different denominations using the same space. The late 16th Duke of Norfolk, being a leading Roman Catholic layman, did a lot to break down the barriers, and as an ecumenical gesture of goodwill, took down the upper part of the wall in 1956; the lower half was removed in 1968. It is now separated by a grille and a glass screen and can only be accessed via the castle. In 1983 the Wilkinson family visited the castle with their children and, whilst the children played on the grassy bank outside, went into the chapel. Suddenly Mrs Wilkinson felt strangely drawn to one of the female effigies in Elizabethan costume on the tomb in one of the side aisles. She turned to tell her husband, but, feeling icy cold and sensing a strong sense of resentment coming from the tomb, he had gone outside. Two friends of the family visited the chapel a few years later, and without knowing of their friends' experience, reported experiencing a cold chill and a feeling of aggressive hostility around the tomb. During the English Civil War the Roundheads used the chapel as a barracks, smashing all the stained glass and mutilating the effigies. It was also used to stable the horses, and some say that this may account for the eerie icy chill experienced by visitors. Another incident occurred in the 1940s when a solicitor took a photograph of the inside of the church, and on receiving the prints was astonished to see 'a shadowy robed figure', possibly that of a priest, standing in front of the altar, although at the time the solicitor was the only person in the church. Over the years there were several reports by the town crier of the figure of a nun in grey habit. Each time she was sitting on a chair but within a few moments would vanish, chair and all! Later the town crier saw the same nun on the stairway of the bell tower, and several years later visitors too reported seeing the apparition. Behind the landing where she was seen was an oak door leading on to a wooden platform, and it's thought that during the Civil War it was used as a lookout point. The nun could have been one of the nuns from the nearby convent order of Poor Clares, who may have jumped or fallen. In January 1975 the 16th duke died, and not long after the funeral one of the church wardens happened to look into the chapel from the St Nicholas side and noticed what he thought was a white-haired family mourner kneeling before the altar. The woman was dressed in a long blue robe and it was not until he mentioned her to the gardener that they realised he had actually seen a ghost! The gardener said the church was locked and only he had a key, and it was still in his pocket. Both men went to check and found the door still locked and no-one inside. One of the most recent sightings occurred in December 1995 when a bell ringer going up the stairs found he was following an unknown person, who disappeared by the time he reached the bell chamber!

❖ BRAMBER ❖

∾ Mystery and legend sit amongst the oak beams ∾

St Mary's House is brimming to its oak beams with intriguing legends and ghosts all living comfortably with its present owners. When Peter Thorogood and Roger Linton combined their finances, talents and skills in 1984 and purchased the medieval house, it already had a long history. Its origins go back to the days of the Knights Templar when Philip de Braose, son of William de Braose of Bramber Castle, went on the First Crusade in 1099, opening up Jerusalem for visiting pilgrims. This led to the founding of the Order of Knights of the Temple of Jerusalem, and when Philip died, his widow bequeathed 5 acres of land at Bramber to the Order. The present building was refashioned around 1470 to accommodate pilgrims on their way to pay homage at the tomb of St Thomas of Canterbury. When Peter moved in he said a monk used to continually knock on the doorway, and it is thought that there is an underground tunnel leading from the house to St Botolph's Monastery at Upper Beeding. Could some long-forgotten monk be knocking to gain admission after a visit? Obviously the monk is content with the restoration as he has been silent for a while. During the Second World War Canadian soldiers billeted at the house reported a mysterious monk wandering about, and land girls reported seeing monks in the vicinity. After the Dissolution of the Monasteries the house was no longer a religious place, and the name dates to the Elizabethan period when it became a grand two-storeyed building. When Queen Elizabeth I visited western Sussex on one of her travels, the most likely place for her to stay would have been with her Treasurer-at-War who lived at nearby Wiston Manor. However, she disliked him, so it's possible that she preferred the hospitality offered at St Mary's. Legend informs us that itinerant painter-stainers were hurriedly hired to decorate the upper chamber with panels depicting scenes of battle with galleons in full sail, believed to be the fleet of King Henry VIII during the battle with the French in 1545. As no records exist, we can't be certain the visit took place, but a photograph of St Mary's taken in 1860 by a Brighton photographer, William Cornish, had the caption 'The house at Bramber at which Queen Elizabeth put up during her summer tour through the south of England.' Several people have reported the smell of musky perfume in the bedroom over the 'Painted Room', and a sweet herby smell like a potpourri has been detected on the landing outside. Strangest of all is the mysterious pretty little Elizabethan child, smartly dressed in doublet and hose with a black velvet hat with a feather, seen playing happily on the upper landing and looking down the stairs in anticipation with a cheeky smile on his face. Is he waiting excitedly for the arrival of the queen? Did he belong to the household of the time, or is he a visitor? If only walls could talk, what stories they would tell. The Edwardian period up to the Great War was a time of splendour for St Mary's with lavish partying and again the years between the two wars were happy with the house now in the hands of the McConnel family, who allowed it to be used as a finishing school for wealthy young American girls. Romantic tales of young men flying over from Shoreham Airport and dropping love-notes into the garden for the girls are all part of its history. One favourite game of the McConnel children was 'The King's Escape' which was played in the King's Room. Behind the chimney-stack there's a secret door, and a hiding place reputed to have been used by Prince Charles prior to his escape to France, verified by the fact that he sailed from Shoreham harbour. Around 1935 Sheelagh McConnel's grandmother, Mimi, several times saw another apparition of a wWhite Lady on the stairs. Who and what is her connection with St Mary's? Obviously these ghosts and their stories are interwoven into the fabric

St Mary's at Bramber has a history reaching back through the centuries (Conrad Hughes)

Was this room hurriedly decorated for Queen Elizabeth I's stay? (Conrad Hughes)

of the building, and like multi-generations living as one family, the ghosts are content to rub shoulders with one another. The owners must feel proud to have saved St Mary's for future generations and have been rewarded by winning several awards, including 'Best Restoration' in Hudson's Heritage Awards 2011; Highly Commended in the Beautiful South Awards for Excellence 2015-16, and the latest, a Highly Commended in the Sussex Heritage Trust Awards 2016. I hope the ghostly family are suitably impressed.

⚜ BREDE ⚜

∾ *What's for supper tonight – a juicy child maybe?* ∾

If tradition can be believed, Brede once had a flesh-eating giant whose speciality was children, and he enjoyed eating one for supper every night. Old Oxenbridge the Ogre, was none other than Sir Goddard Oxenbridge of Brede Place. However, history tells a tale of a good Christian who was an usher at the funeral of Henry VII and made a Knight of the Bath to honour the coronation of Henry VIII. But, let's return to folklore. It's said that 'neither bow and arrow, nor axe, nor sword, nor spear, could slay this redoubtable giant', but he was finally brought down by

The tomb of Sir Goddard Oxenbridge, a good man or an eater of children? (Conrad Hughes)

a group of children who brewed a huge vat of beer and placed it on Groaning Bridge. Unable to resist, the giant soon drank every drop, watched from a distance by the children. Once he was hopelessly drunk they sawed him in half with a wooden saw, the East Sussex children one end, their West Sussex cousins the other. The spot is haunted by his ghost in the form of a severed tree. A true tale or not? We shall never know, but theories are many. The story may have originated because Sir Goddard was a Catholic at a time when they were unpopular, or smugglers occupying Brede Place may have used the tale to prevent nosy people from prying. Some have suggested local mothers created the story to encourage naughty children to behave.

✢ BOSHAM ✢

✎ *Who lies beneath?* ✎

The palace of King Canute at Bosham is featured on the Bayeux Tapestry, and the distraught king was said to have buried his 8-year-old daughter in the church near where she tragically drowned in a mill stream, but with little evidence to back the story of his daughter, it remained a myth. Then in 1865, the *Gentleman's*

Magazine carried a report that a coffin containing a child's skeleton had been discovered in what is now the chancel. The coffin, assumed to be that of the little princess, was covered with a slab of stone 7 inches thick, and contained a 3ft 9in skeleton, wearing no jewellery or personal possessions, so the mystery remained unsolved. In 1954 the Victorian flooring needed to be replaced, and close to the little girl's coffin, a second beautifully carved Saxon coffin was discovered, containing the skeleton of a stocky man, about 5ft 6in tall, aged over 60 with an arthritic hip and pelvic joints. It was first thought to be that of Goodwin, Earl of Wessex, but he and King Canute are buried at Winchester. The elaborate coffin would suggest he was of great importance, but why was he buried so close the King Canute's daughter?

Memorial to King Canute's daughter who may be buried in Bosham (Conrad Hughes)

⚜ BROADWATER ⚜

∾ *Who's Molly?* ∾

When Molly Corbett died at the age of 15 her parents chose to lay her to rest at Broadwater, and erect a beautiful monument in her memory. It's the finest in the cemetery, and depicts a statue of Our Lady of Grace, head bowed, hands outstretched, but little is known of the family or its connections with the area. Records give Molly's age as 16, and she died at Lausanne in Switzerland on 5 January 1928, where she was finishing her education. Why then did it take her parents until 13 May 1929, a full sixteen months later, to bury her? Was there some mysterious circumstance surrounding her death that needed to be cleared up first? Her father Maxwell Campbell Corbett was born in 1888, and the family lived in Malaysia, and later burial records tell us he was a mining engineer who died in Mexico City and joined Molly in the family tomb on 30 June 1947, some thirty months after his death. Eileen Kathleen Veronica Corbett, his widow, died in Brisbane, Australia in May 1985, aged 87, and joined Molly and her husband in the family vault in June that year. Grave diggers at the time reported that the

Who is Molly and what are her connections with Broadwater? (Conrad Hughes)

vault is fully tiled and Molly is interred in a glass coffin. The Friends of Broadwater and Worthing Cemetery have carried out much research but failed to find any connection between this obviously wealthy family and the area, and for now it remains a mystery.

⚘ BROADBRIDGE HEATH ⚘

⁓ *Strangled, burned and then hanged* ⁓

Anne Waterton was christened in Horsham in 1731, and her parents William and Elizabeth had five daughters and a son. William was an upright member of the community who provided a good education, appropriate for children of a burgess and butcher. He also kept the Sign and Cock Inn, just two doors from the famous gaol where his daughter would be held before her 21st birthday. She was still a young girl when her father died, but her mother continued the business and did the best for the family. Anne was erratic and disobedient, and after an argument with her mother went completely off the rails, ran away and kept bad company. Eventually to save her from ruin her mother brought her home and Anne settled down. To prevent her slipping back, Elizabeth thought marriage to a respectable man would be ideal. We can imagine how pleased she must have felt when a customer, good honest labourer James Whale, took an interest in Anne, and deciding to take advantage of the situation, Elizabeth gave the couple her consent and blessing, and they married in September 1749. Anne and James moved to Chiltington, then to Pulborough, before settling in August 1750 in part of a rented house known as Corsett's on Broadbridge Heath. The other part of the house was rented by James and Sarah Pledge, an older cousin of Anne's, but very soon James Whale fell out with Sarah and banished her from his part of the house. On her 21st birthday in June 1752 Anne was to inherit £80 from an uncle, and this may have been the motive for what followed. With James around Sarah had little chance of persuading Anne to give her a share of the money, but one day when James was at work, Sarah visited Anne and, fuelled by the quarrel and upset at not being able to gain from the money, Sarah is quoted as saying, 'Nan, I say, let us get rid of this devil.' They agreed on poison and Sarah set out to find some, but couldn't obtain any locally or at Dorking. She considered asking Mr Harfoy, an apothecary who lived next to the King's Head in Horsham, but thought it too close to home, so resorted to folklore. She made a potion using spiders, which she put in a glass mixed with a little beer, and baked them before putting the mixture into a bottle of beer, for James to drink. Anne had second thoughts, and without telling Sarah she threw the bottle away. Puzzled that James had not been violently sick, Sarah threw caution to the wind, and set off once more to buy a pennyworth of white mercury from Mr Halfoy. On her return she made a pudding laced with the mercury and served it up to James. Half an hour later he became ill, and died the following morning. During his inquest it was claimed that 'James Whale by the visitation of Almighty God, came by his death', and so the women thought they had got away with murder. However, not long after the funeral, John Agate, who owned Corsett's, called on Mr Halfoy who innocently asked if he'd managed to get rid of the rats. Suspicious, Agate went to the authorities, and consequently Sarah and Anne were arrested and taken to Horsham goal, where Anne spent her 21st birthday. At the trial the women blamed each other, but the judge decided they were both guilty and sentenced Sarah to be hanged. Anne was found guilty of *petit treason*, judged to be a worse crime than murder, and was sentenced to burning at the stake, but as an act of humanity she would be strangled before the fire was lit. On 24 July 1752, a month after Anne should have inherited, the pair were taken to Broadbridge Heath Common, Sarah in a cart and Anne on a sledge. At 3.30 p.m. Sarah was hanged, and two hours later Anne was led to the stake, chained to the post, strangled, and the fire lit. As the initial flames died down her skeleton could be seen. Sarah's body was taken down, put in a tallow-chandler's hamper and taken to Storrington for dissection.

BRIGHTON

Inventor of vapour baths

Sake Dean Mahomed, a Bengali traveller, became one of the most notable non-European immigrants to the Western world. He was born in India in 1759, where his father was employed by the East India Company. His father died when he was only 10-years-old, and the next year he joined the East India Company, and soon found a father-figure in Captain Godfrey Evan Baker, an Anglo-Irish officer who treated him like a son. He served in the British East India Company Army as a trainee surgeon, and remained with Captain Baker's unit until the captain retired in 1782. After thirteen years' service Mahomed chose to leave the army and accompany his 'best friend' to Ireland, where Captain Baker paid for him to study English language and literature at a local school. Here Mahomed fell in love with Jane Daly, a respectable Irish woman, but her family strongly opposed the relationship. Mahomed decided to convert from Islam to Protestantism, but because it was illegal for Protestants and Catholics to marry the couple eloped. Mahomed moved his young growing family to London in search of opportunities, but instead of settling amongst the merchants who traded with India he moved to Portman Square, the hub of high society. His first job was as an assistant to Sir Basil Cochrane, who had installed a steam bath in his home in Portman Square for public use and promoted its medical benefits, and Mahomed was responsible for introducing the practice of 'champoo' (Indian Massage) which became anglicised

An 1826 illustration of Mohomed's Baths on Brighton's sea front

to shampooing. The treatment involved the patient first lying in an herbal steam bath, and when sweating being placed in a flannel tent with sleeves. Outside the tent the practitioner would put his arms through the sleeves and administer the massage. In his fifties Mahomed moved his family to Brighton but the only work he could find was as a manager of a bathhouse, so here branded himself the Inventor of the Indian Medicated Vapour Baths. Cashing in on his Indian heritage he added the title Sake (a variation of Sheik) to his name, and opened the first 'shampooing' vapour masseur bath in England on the site now occupied by the Queen's Hotel. His treatments were described in a local paper as the Indian Medicated Vapour Bath (a type of Turkish bath), a cure for many diseases and giving relief to such things as rheumatic, gout, stiff joints, lame legs and aches and pains of the joints. He became an instant success, with hospitals referring patients to him. He was also appointed shampooing surgeon to both King George IV and William IV. Mahomed was also a generous donor to local charities and became the official steward for the annual charity ball, dressing in a costume modelled on the Mughal court dress. In 1851, just two months after Jane died, he passed away at the age of 92, at home at 32 Grand Parade, Brighton and is buried in a grave in St Nicholas's Church, Brighton.

∞ *She fooled the army* ∞

Not many people can claim the accolade of living through the reign of several monarchs, but Phoebe Hessel, born in 1713 in the reign of Queen Anne, died during the reign of George IV, aged 108. At the age of 15 she fell in love with Samuel Golding, a dashing soldier. When he was posted to the West Indies she disguised herself as a man and enlisted in the Fifth Regiment of Foot, to be with him. They served alongside each other in the West Indies and Gibraltar, and in 1745 fought under the Duke of Cumberland at the Battle of Fountenoy, where she received a bayonet wound in the arm. When Samuel was injured in the same battle and invalided home, Phoebe, after seventeen years of army life, revealed her sex to the wife of the regiment's colonel, and was discharged without punishment. Samuel was honourably discharged with full pay. The couple married and lived in

Phoebe Hessel who tricked the army,
and lived to be 108

Phoebe's grave, restored
by the Northumberland
Fusiliers (Conrad Hughes)

Plymouth where they had nine children, but eight died in infancy., The surviving
child reached adulthood, but died at sea. They were married for twenty years, and
when Samuel died Phoebe moved to Brighton where she met and married a
fisherman, Thomas Hessel. By the time he died Phoebe had become something of
a character, telling her tales of army life, no doubt embellished with each telling,

to anyone in a crowded bar willing to listen and give her a few pennies. Local friends gave her a donkey and she used it to hawk fish around the neighbourhood to support herself. Later on she had to resort to selling gingerbread, apples and oranges on a street corner near the Pavilion but, unable to support herself, she was taken into the workhouse, but discharged herself in August 1806. Her story and her great age came to the attention of the Prince Regent, and in 1808 he granted her a pension of half a guinea a week which was paid to her until she died. The prince called her a jolly old fellow, and on hearing the news of her pension, she replied, 'That will make me as happy as a princess.' As the oldest inhabitant of the town, she attended the coronation of George IV in July 1821, sharing a carriage with the vicar of Brighton, and was guest of honour at the town's banquet. In December that year Phoebe passed away and was buried in St Nicholas's churchyard. In the 1970s her grave was restored by the Northumberland Fusiliers, successors to Phoebe's regiment.

⚜ BRIGHTLING ⚜

∾ *Crazy Building Jack* ∾

If John 'Mad Jack' Fuller wished to be remembered, then he achieved his aim. A pyramid is not what you'd expect to see in a local Sussex churchyard, but during his lifetime 'Mad Jack' scattered the area around Brightling with a series of 'over the top' landmarks, and built walls simply to keep the locals in employment. His grand mausoleum in the churchyard of St Thomas à Becket was erected some twenty-three years before he died. It was always said that the portly 22 stone Jack, also known as Hippopotamus, was buried inside the tomb, sitting in an armchair, before a table set with a meal of chicken and a bottle of claret by his hand and wearing a top hat and tails. Broken glass is strewn across the floor to prevent the Devil from taking him. A great story, but during renovations in 1982 when the door was replaced with a grille, Jack was found buried in a conventional manner under a marble slab. It is said that the site of his pyramid was once occupied by the Green Man public house, and when Jack asked the vicar for permission to build his mausoleum, the vicar immediately agreed, on condition the pub was taken down and moved half a mile up the road. He had become concerned that folk, including his own bell ringers, were spending too much time in the pub on a Sunday. On his twentieth birthday Jack inherited the family estates and a large fortune, amassed through vast sugar plantations in Jamaica and the smelting and manufacturing of iron goods, including weapons. He became MP for Lewes twice, but retired from politics when he disgraced himself in Parliament. In a drunken state during a debate about France, he called the Speaker of the House, 'The insignificant little fellow in the wig.' Although a larger than life character he had no pretensions and

Jack Fuller pyramid
grave in St Thomas
à Becket churchyard
(Conrad Hughes)

Brightling Needle, built
to celebrate Wellington's
victory over Napoleon
(Conrad Hughes)

when William Pitt offered him a peerage he refused saying, 'I was born Jack Fuller, and I'll die Jack Fuller.' However, he acquired the nickname 'Mad Jack', not because he was mad, but due of his extravagant spending habits. For example he built an obelisk, or Brightling Needle, to celebrate Wellington's victory over Napoleon. Next came a working observatory built after he was inspired by the king's private astronomer, Sir William Herschel. Another of his building endeavours, which now sits in the middle of Brightling Park, is the Rotunda Temple, which came about when, making improvements to Jack's estate, the well-known landscape gardener Humphrey Repton suggested building a temple. Usually Fuller rejected any of his suggestions, but obviously the idea of a temple appealed to him, so it was built. Tradition informs us that Jack used to hold gambling sessions and wild parties in the temple, and entertained the ladies. It also contains an underground store where he kept wine. Opposite the park can be seen another of his efforts, a circular two-storey tower which was inspired when Fuller was restoring Bodiam Castle.

⚜ BULVERHYTHE ⚜

ꙮ *Wrecked on our shores* ꙮ

The *Amsterdam's* story begins in the port of Amsterdam in 1748 when she was built, resembling a warship, for the East India Company. Her captain, Willem Klump, was 33, and lived with his wife and young son in a smart house overlooking the Prinsengracht in the city. Her maiden voyage was to Batavia, the then capital city

The wreck of the *Amsterdam* at Bulverhythe visible at low tide (Shipwreck and Heritage Centre, Hastings)

Wine bottles
recovered from
the *Amsterdam*
(Conrad Hughes)

of the Dutch East Indies, now Jakarta. Willem, an experienced sailor, was fully aware of the dangers that a nine-month voyage entailed. On board, the cargo of textiles, wine, stone ballast, cannon, paper, pens, pipes, domestic goods and twenty-seven chests of silver guilders, worth several millions of pounds in today's money, was to be sold in China, Japan and Indonesia. On her return voyage she would bring back precious silks, spices, and porcelain destined for the European market. In November a crew of 203 and 125 soldiers, one male and two female passengers boarded the ship at Texel but, because of high winds and a number of false starts, the *Amsterdam* didn't actually leave until 8 January 1749. It was not an easy voyage, and weeks into the expedition fifty of the crew members died of an unknown disease, forty became sick, and as she entered the English Channel the *Amsterdam* encountered a strong gale at Pevensey, and struck the seabed, tearing her rudder. The crew wanted to steer the ship on to the shoreline and wait until the gale subsided, but Captain Klump sailed on regardless, hoping to reach Portsmouth. After a row the crew staged a mutiny, and broke into the cargo of wine. Finally the ship came ashore on Sunday afternoon, 26 January, at Bulverhythe Bay. A crowd of spectators and looters were quickly on the scene, and by morning the throng had increased to over 1,000. Using long poles with hooks attached, they stole items of value off the ship. The crew were brought off the ship, and the Dutchmen were lowered over the side and given medical help before returning to the Netherlands. The Mayor of Hastings placed a guard of soldiers around the ship, and the silver coinage was removed for safekeeping by the local authority. Soon the soldiers and the villagers and even the salvage workers began looting, and by March all hopes of salvage were called off. Captain Klump returned to the Netherlands, exonerated of any blame, and the file on the *Amsterdam* was closed. She remained forgotten, until a low spring tide in 1969 exposed several decks. Archaeologist Dr Peter Marsden carried out the first survey of the wreck and when bottles full of wine, bronze guns and a large variety of objects were found he advised on further excavation. The site became a designated protected site under the Protection of Wrecks Act on 5 February 1974, and diving on to it or recovering any artefacts was forbidden. In 1975 a Save the *Amsterdam* Foundation was established in the Netherlands, and using a Dutch-British team of divers and archaeologists they uncovered part of the lower gun deck. Due to the mutiny the ship had been left in chaos, with books, food remains, medical equipment and clothing strewn across the deck. Interestingly some of the artefacts were able to be linked to their owners; for example, two sisters who survived the shipwreck were Pieternella and Catharina Schook, and on aboard they left a fine dress and part of the quilted petticoat decorated with hearts and flowers, some high-heeled shoes and a spoon with the initials PBS – Pietermella Bockom Schook. Eventually the Dutch plan is to raise the *Amsterdam* and take her back to her birthplace, but for now she remains protruding out of the sand at low spring tides.

⁂ BUXTED ⁂

ᔕ *Was Nan a murderess or a witch?* ᔕ

Nan Tuck may not have been treated well by her peers, but whilst they are all forgotten, Nan lives on in a lane named after her. For some reason she poisoned her husband, but within a few days her crime was discovered. Village fingers pointed at Nan, who lived in a cottage on the edge of the wood, and as this was a time of ignorance, superstition and fear, Nan was branded a witch. She decided to seek refuge in a church, knowing that if she could touch the altar, she might evade punishment. With renewed courage, she fled down the lane towards the church, but she was too late; the local officials and the villagers were hot on her heels, and with nowhere to go the exhausted Nan ran into the woods, hiding in hedges and haystacks. Her followers were now sure she would not escape, but then a strange thing happened; she just mysteriously vanished. Anyone visiting the woods today will discover a circular patch of earth completely barren of vegetation. Is this the place where Nan met her demise? Many motorists have reported seeing a ghostly figure of a lady clad in dark grey, gliding down the lane in the dead of night. But there is another story which is more appalling. Some say she suffered the indignity of trial by water, and half-drowned, bedraggled and terrified, she managed to escape. Her tormentors gave chase, but she was found hanging from a tree. Was it suicide or murder? Unfortunately we may never the truth, but poor Nan Tuck's name lives on.

⚜ CHANCTONBURY RING ⚜

∞ *Strange goings-on on the top* ∞

Chanctonbury Ring must be the most mysterious and atmospheric place in Sussex. It has more legends and folklore attached to it than anywhere else in the county. It is claimed that the sixteenth-century astrologer and druid Prince Agasicles Synnesis, a frequent visitor, died in the ring after writing, in charcoal, 'Bury me where I have fallen', Once an Iron Age fort, the Romans must have considered it pretty special as they erected two temples there, but when they left in the fourth century it remained unoccupied, used only for grazing cattle. In 1750, in order to make it look beautiful, 20-year-old Charles Goring, landowner of nearby Wiston House, planted a ring of beech trees around the top. He watered them daily until the roots took hold, and living to 85 he saw them mature, but the trees in the middle of the ring never grew well and everyone wondered why, until a Roman temple was discovered. Many of the trees were destroyed during the storm of 1987, and today a low fence protects the replacement trees. Legend tells us the ring was created by the Devil himself, and if you venture to the top and run around the ring seven times on May Day, Midsummer's Eve or any other moonlit night you will see the Devil. He will offer you a bowl of milk, soup or porridge, but there is a condition. If you accept, you must walk around the ring widdershins, or backwards. In return he'll take your soul. If you only make it around the ring three times, an apparition of a lady on a white horse will appear. Countless investigators and walkers have heard and seen a variety of strange happenings ranging from a crying baby to chanting monks. In the 1930s it became the in place to visit, with Southern Railway running special excursions. Some mediums have even been attacked at the ring and had the fingermarks to prove it. In August 1974, four men from the Ghost and Psychic Investigations Group decided to spend the night at the top, but as they walked to the centre one was lifted several feet off the ground, and suspended in mid-air. In pain he kept crying out, 'No more, No more!' Finally, exhausted, he dropped to the floor, landing heavily on his back. Strange voices belonging to no-one in the group were captured on digital recorders, and some have experienced sudden bouts of unexplained sickness and disorientation. Even

Walking to the top of Chanctonbury Ring (West Sussex Library)

horses shy away from the top, and sounds of thundering hooves and the beat of drums have been heard, accompanied by the ghost of a man on a horse galloping past without stopping. Some say it is Julius Caesar and his army.

⚛ CHIDDINGLY ⚛

∞ *How about another piece of your favourite pie?* ∞

When John was called to his brother's home at twenty past midnight on 8 January 1852 he found his sister-in-law, Sarah Ann, in the living room in tears being comforted by the neighbours. William and Sarah Ann had been married for seven years and lived in a cottage near the Gunn Inn with their young son. The two brothers were hard-working labourers on Stream Farm, and the last time John had seen William was on Christmas Eve, and he was in good health. Even before John arrived the village tongues were wagging as to the cause of a perfectly healthy man's sudden demise. With growing concern, the local constable was called and ordered the body to be exhumed for a post-mortem. Three days after William died the body was examined by a surgeon, who suspected poisoning and retained samples of the stomach and intestines for testing. Traces of arsenic were found.

Twenty-seven-year-old Sarah had earned a reputation as a loving wife, caring mother and good neighbour, but she had fallen in love with a younger man, 20-year-old James Hickman. Only one person stood between her and a life of happiness, or so she thought. Her crime of passion became known as the Onion Pie Murder, because Sarah laced William's favourite supper dish of onion pie with a lethal dose of arsenic, which apparently is sweet, and goes undetected when mixed with onion and garlic. James Hickman had been going out with Sarah's sister Jane, but the couple split up. He visited Sarah on the pretext of reading stories to her son, who had been ill, and Sarah made it clear that she was attracted to him. If William was at work, she would sit on his knee and kiss him, and told him she had £500 tucked away, and if she ever became single again she would marry him. Sarah was arrested and charged with William's murder and sentenced to death. In a state of collapse she was led from the dock, but by the time she had returned to Lewes gaol she had recovered. Her death warrant was received on Wednesday 7 April, and the 'New Drop' gallows began to be erected in front of the gaol on the Thursday. On Saturday 10 April the scaffold was draped in black, and could be seen towering above the wall of the goal. By 9 a.m. a crowd had already assembled, and soon trains arrived from various parts of the country bringing even more spectators. Around seven minutes to midday a bell rang out from the gaol to indicate they were ready, and Sarah appeared wearing a dress of drab material, and a cap drawn over her head. She was placed under the beam and the rope put around her neck. Calcroft the executioner, wearing a sombre black suit, went below, and withdrew the bolt holding the stage. Sarah fought hard for two or three minutes, then became still as a huge crowd estimated at between 3 and 4,000 watched. Her body hung for an hour before it was taken down for burial within the prison grounds.

❖ CUCKFIELD ❖

∞ *The sleeping maid* ∞

No doubt after a long day, a most peculiar event took place at Marshalls Manor, the home of Mr and Mrs Woods. One of their female servants fell asleep in the attic bedroom, and proceeded to sleep and sleep and sleep! In fact she slept continuously for the next eight days. Her worried employers tried everything to arouse her, and in sheer desperation called the village doctor, but he could find no apparent reason for her deep dormant state, except that her body temperature had dropped. There was nothing her employers could do other than wait and see what transpired. A week later, having suffered no ill effects, the servant girl woke to the sound of the church bells. She rubbed the sleep from her eyes and said she was 'sorry her indisposition had caused her to lie beyond her ordinary hour.' Thankfully she had suffered no ill effects, but the tale has become legendary.

∞ *Eating to extreme* ∞

The *Sussex Weekly Advertiser* reported in 1797 an odd story of a flax-dresser who accepted a wager. He claimed he could eat his way through a square foot (about 42 lbs) of plum pudding in a fortnight. A number of bets were placed on the outcome, and the villagers eagerly wanted to see if he could do it. A week later, feeling very sick indeed, the man decided he would carry on, and tucked into 4 lbs of pudding at his seventh meal. To make it more interesting he varied the flavour by adding some mustard and vinegar, but a day later his jaws refused to work and he was forced to give in.

CROWBOROUGH

∞ *Chased by a bag of soot* ∞

One of the most bizarre ghostly encounters must be in the vicinity of Jarvis Brook Road. During the nineteenth century, the area was haunted by a bag of soot of all things. On certain nights the mischievous bag would appear and pursue people down the road. A blacksmith once boasted in the village inn that he wasn't scared of any silly bag of soot, and suitably encouraged and fortified with drink, he set off for home, his companions waiting at the foot of the hill for the outcome. Soon he came running down the road, chased by the bag of soot, and ran straight past his friends and into his house and bolted himself in. Why a bag of soot? Some suggest that it could be the spirit of a long-deceased chimney sweep, annoyed by the people of Jarvis Brook who used the old Sussex tradition of cleaning a chimney by creating a fire instead of using a chimney sweep. We can assume that with the advent of central heating the spirit is now at peace, because there haven't been any recent sightings in the area.

✤ DALLINGTON ✤

∞ *Just to win his bet* ∞

The iconic Sugarloaf was erected by the same 'Mad Jack' Fuller we met at Brightling, and so named because at the time sugar was sold in that shape. One night Jack was at a party in London and boasted that from his house, Rose Hill, he could see the spire of St Giles church at Dallington. Arriving home he realised that this wasn't true, so Jack immediately ordered workmen to erect a 40ft replica of the spire on the nearby hill, giving the illusion of a half-visible church. Obviously it must have cost him a great deal more than the bet to have it built, one of the many reasons he acquired his nickname, but he was also known for engaging out-of-work men to build, simply to give them employment. The Sugarloaf was actually used as a two-storey dwelling up until the 1930s, and considering that it is only 15ft (4.57m) in diameter it must have been a very tight squeeze for one person, let alone Simeon Crouch and his family who lived there in the late 1870s. It has windows on each floor and a ladder to take you from one level to another. It also had a small lean-to kitchen, and during the Second World War, was used as an anti-invasion machine-gun post, but by the mid 1950s it had fallen into disrepair, and when Dennis Baker bought Christmas Farm, on which the Sugarloaf stands, he donated it to East Sussex County Council.

Mad Jack's Sugarloaf, built to honour a bet
(Conrad Hughes)

⁙ DRAGON'S GREEN ⁙

∞ *When is a tombstone not a grave?* ∞

Passing through Dragon's Green you may stop and wonder why there's a memorial standing outside a public house. The son of Alfred and Charlotte Budd, then landlords of the pub, was born albino. There wasn't much sympathy for or understanding of such things in those days, and sadly, instead of being accepted by his peers, Walter became the constant victim of ridicule, not helped by the fact that he was also an epileptic. Constant jibes and taunting played on Walter's mind, but when he was accused of petty theft, this was the last straw. He finally cracked under the strain, went down to the river and drowned himself. His distraught parents buried him in nearby Shipley churchyard and erected a marble cross bearing the words:

> *In loving memory of Walter, the Albino son of Alfred and Charlotte Budd.*
> *Born February 12th 1867. Died February 19th 1893.*
> *May God forgive those who forgot their duty to him who was just and afflicted.*

The George and Dragon with its unusual memorial (Conrad Hughes)

The vicar, the Rev. Gorham, was outraged at the final sentence and demanded the removal of the memorial immediately. Walter's parents thought for a while, and then, since it was a free house not restricted by brewery regulations, they decided to place the cross together with a note explaining their actions outside their pub. Not long afterwards the Rev. Arkle took over the parish, and he too found the situation troubling and ordered the removal of two wreaths that had been placed on the unmarked grave by grieving friends. Again his parents retaliated, by adding to the note outside their pub, which read:

> *This cross was erected on the grave in Shipley churchyard and removed by order of H Gorham, vicar. Two globe wreaths were placed on the grave by friends, and after being there for two years were removed by E Arkle, the following vicar.*

The memorial is still outside today as a memorial of the undying love his parents had for their son.

⁙ DITCHLING ⁙

∞ *If only it hadn't rained* ∞

Jacob Harris, an itinerant Jewish peddler, might have got away with his crime if it hadn't been for a sudden downpour. Yacob Hirch, alias Jacob Harris, peddled odds and ends to the cottagers and could also be seen selling from a stall at the three-day Fair of St Margaret of Antioch in Ditchling. Although homeless, he often stopped at an inn overnight for a decent meal and to clean up. Everyone knew him, in his distinctive bottle-green ankle-length coat and large-brimmed hat. When he was in the area he would stay at the Royal Oak pub, although the landlord Richard Miles was suspicious of him, because whenever he stayed items of clothing would go missing. One particular evening sitting in the bar drinking his ale, he overheard Richard bragging that business was good and he'd made a clear £20 profit that week. Some say that the cash was the motive for the crime, but early the following morning when Richard went to attend to the peddler's horse in the stables, he caught Jacob stealing his best riding cape worth ten shillings. On seeing the landlord, Jacob drew his knife and slashed Miles's throat twice. On hearing the commotion, a serving girl went to see what was going on, and before she could escape Jacob stabbed her, leaving her bloodstained body draped over the banister. By now Dorothy the landlady had opened the bedroom door, and seeing the girl's body, locked herself in her bedroom, but Jacob smashed the door, and stabbed her too. Before leaving he robbed the house and fled with his ill-gotten gains to the Cat, in West Hoathly, 15 miles away and a well-known smugglers' haunt. Meanwhile Richard was able to whisper the name of the murderer. Word spread fast, so Jacob moved on to Selsfield House at Turners Hill, thinking he would be safe, but the weather changed suddenly, bringing rain and strong winds. The conditions made it hard for the men out looking for him, but John Oliver was determined to get his man, and defiantly waded through the mud and persistent drizzle in pursuit of the peddler. He stopped at every tavern he came across, to break the news before asking if anyone had seen Jacob. When he arrived at Selsfield House, Jacob saw the men pass the window and hid in the wide chimney in the parlour used by smugglers. He thought he would be safe, but the officers arrived drenched and hungry and asked for the fire to be lit in the parlour to dry their uniforms. As the men settled around the fire, much to their surprise there was a tremendous coughing and spluttering coming from inside the chimney, and a blackened Jacob tumbled at their feet. He tried to get away, but after a fierce struggle was captured. Meanwhile Richard Miles died four days later. Harris was taken to Horsham Gaol, and tried for his crimes. He pleaded not guilty, and was acquitted of housebreaking, but found guilty of triple murder. The following Sunday, 31 August 1743, after an impressive sermon by Mr Healey, he was hanged at Horsham gaol and his body was taken down, gibbeted and hung on Ditchling Common near the Royal Oak to deter others. The post itself took on a life of its own as it was said that to touch the post would cure any ailment and any 'believer' who visited the pub could find a small part of the original gibbet hanging on the wall. This continued well into the nineteenth century, although the original post had been replaced and a metal rooster attached to the top. Many might think that would have been the end of the tragic tale, but the voice of the serving girl could still be heard in the rear corridor of the pub, screaming, 'Mr Miles, Mr Miles …'

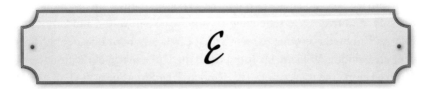

⊹ EARTHAM ⊹

∞ *The first railway fatality* ∞

The 15 September 1830 was to be an exciting day for William Huskisson, MP for Chichester, and his wife Emily. Instead the MP is remembered as the first railway fatality, struck by one of Stephenson's 'Rocket' engines. William was influential in the creation of the British Empire, but fell out with the Duke of Wellington over an issue of free trade, particularly concerning the Corn Laws, and resigned from Cabinet. William had been invited to the grand opening of the Liverpool and Manchester Railway and as he knew the Duke was going, he hoped for reconciliation. There were eight inaugural trains running on the line that day, with

Eartham House, now Great Ballard School, former home of William Huskisson, the first railway victim. (Conrad Hughes)

Wellington's special train, carrying the Duke and the Prime Minister, on one track, and the other seven on adjacent tracks. At Parkside Station, the midpoint of the line, the locomotives were scheduled to stop to take in water, and although the railway staff advised everyone to stay in their carriages, about fifty people decided to get out, including William. He had spotted the Duke sitting in the front carriage, and walked along the track to offer his hand in friendship, but as the Duke reached out his hand, the crowd noticed the Rocket hauling the third train approaching on the other track. 'Engine approaching,' they shouted in desperation. The driver of the Rocket, Joseph Locke, threw the engine into reverse, as William desperately tried to enter the Duke's carriage, but the door flew open leaving him hanging in the path of the Rocket. To everyone's horror, the engine passed over his leg and for a minute he watched his shaking leg. 'It's all over for me,' he said. 'Bring me my wife and let me die.' A spectator laid his coat over the damaged leg and Emily was brought to his side. Passengers took the door off a storeroom and lifted William on to the makeshift stretcher, before placing him in the flat-bottomed wagon of the Duke's train and, with George Stephenson driving, they set off for Manchester. Joseph Brandeth, a Liverpool surgeon and fellow passenger, believed William was dying and suggested they stop at the first house they came to. Four miles short of Manchester they stopped at a vicarage where William was given laudanum and brandy and his clothing cut to reveal the full extent of his injury. By 4 p.m. he'd rallied enough to dictate a brief amendment to his will ensuring that Emily inherited his property, but his condition worsened and he passed away that evening. Emily returned to a quiet life, keeping her husband's memory alive.

⚜ EASTBOURNE ⚜

∞ *The parachute queen* ∞

Although Dolly Shepherd's ballooning career only lasted eight years, she packed in enough thrilling adventures to last a lifetime, until one day in 1912, during a solo ascent, she heard a voice telling her to stop or she would be killed. Dolly listened and stopped. In later life she settled down and spent her last twenty years in Eastbourne. She was christened Elizabeth Miriam, but everyone called her Dolly. At the age of 16 she took a job as a waitress at Alexandra Palace in London so that she could see the composer John Philip Sousa whom she greatly admired. She enjoyed taking risks, and while working there volunteered to stand in on a shooting act for the showman Samuel Franklin Cody, nicknamed the Colonel, who was touring England from America. Cody's wife was his usual assistant but one evening he'd grazed the top of her head and the show had to be cancelled. Dolly ended up spending a year as his target, until one day he took her to see the workshop of Auguste Gaudron, a French parachutist and balloonist. Gaudron casually asked Dolly if she would like to make a parachute jump, and within half an hour Cody lost his assistant and Dolly became a trainee parachutist. It was a dangerous occupation; the safety harness was yet to be invented, and the parachute was no more than a canvas canopy, with a small air-filled balloon hanging below. The parachutist would jump off a trapeze bar to enable the parachute to open. Dolly took her occupation seriously and even designed her own costume, a navy blue suit with gold trimmings, and as she sat on her trapeze bar she would wave a Union Jack handkerchief to the crowd. In 1905 Dolly made her first performance jump with thousands of people watching. But it wasn't always an easy ride, and on one occasion both the balloon and the parachute failed, and she found herself rising to 15,000 ft. She lost her grip due to the cold and lack of oxygen, and would have plummeted to the ground, but thankfully the balloon sank to earth some three and a half hours later. However, her luck nearly ran out in July 1908 when a new jumper, Louie May, was due to make her debut descent from one of Gaudron's Mammoth balloons, but he felt the wind was too strong and refused to let her jump, promising the crowd she would jump the next day. That evening Dolly joined them after performing in Ashby-de-la-Zouch, and the decision was taken for them to do a double jump. The next day brought better weather, but the Mammoth balloon developed a fault and collapsed. Dolly had brought her small balloon with her, and it was just big enough to lift the two girls. It took a while to rig the two parachutes up, one on each side for balance, and by 8 p.m. they were ready. A roar went up from the jubilant crowd, but it was short-lived. Louie's parachute wouldn't release and Dolly tried to use the rope connecting the trapeze to pull them together, but without success. Level-headed Dolly carefully released Louie's harness, telling her to wrap her arms and legs around her so they could descend safely on the one parachute. However, the descent was too fast and they landed in a field. Louie's landing was cushioned by Dolly, but Dolly had injured her back and was taken to a nearby farmhouse where she remained for eight weeks. A London back specialist was sent for and told her she'd never walk again, and began to make arrangements for her to be admitted to a hospital for incurables. Meanwhile, a local doctor used a mild electric shock treatment which enabled her to move her legs again, and within a few weeks Dolly not only learnt to walk again but gained a place as the Guinness World Record holder for the first mid-air rescue. Two years later another jump was planned, but again fate intervened. It was arranged for 9 July 1910 at Coventry, but at the last minute Edith Maud Cook took her place. Her parachute collapsed in a gust of wind and she landed on a factory roof before a second gust caught the parachute. Edith fell off the roof and died on 14 July from multiple injuries. According to *BBC History Magazine* Dolly liked to 'go high' because 'I have it in my head that if I had to be killed, I'd like to be killed completely: good and proper!' She recalled that on one occasion she almost landed on a steam train, but the driver had the presence of mind to blow the steam and she ended up in a canal. Now retired from ballooning, and four days into the First World War, Dolly and her sister joined the Women's Emergency Corps, later to become the Women's Volunteer Reserve, and by the summer of 1915 she was driving a munitions truck for the War Department. In 1917 Dolly volunteered for overseas duties as a driver/mechanic in France, where women weren't welcomed, but once they showed their mechanical and driving expertise, and willingness to work long hours, they began to be valued. No stranger to danger, Dolly once carried a live shell in the boot of a car until it could be detonated. She also suffered frostbite and a surgeon had to replace two of her toes on each foot with those from an amputated foot. She also chauffeured officers and one person she was required to drive was rent and lands officer Captain Sedgwick. At first he objected strongly to having a woman driver, but when he came to know Dolly better their friendship grew, and eventually they married. During the Second World War she worked on the home front in Lewisham and was commended for her war efforts by the *News Chronicle* in the 1940s. After the war the couple moved to the Isle of Wight where her husband died in 1956, and later in 1963 she moved to Eastbourne. In 1976 she was invited to join the Parachute Red Devils, and greatly admired modern techniques in parachuting. At the grand age of 90 she flew with the Red Devils as they gave a display over Worthing. She died in 1983 at Eastbourne, just short of her 97th birthday. Both the Red Devils and the RAF Falcons were represented at her funeral, and the *Eastbourne Herald* reported that she was 'one of the most intrepid, charming and colourful characters ever to have lived in Eastbourne'. She has a bench dedicated to her opposite the Grand Hotel: *In Loving Memory of Elizabeth Sedgwick (1886–1983) Dolly Shepherd Pioneer Aeronaut/Balloonist 1904–1912.*

Dolly wearing the navy costume she designed with gold trimmings and holding her Union Jack handkerchief

Bench in memory of Dolly Shepherd
opposite the Grand Hotel in Eastbourne
(Conrad Hughes)

⁜ EAST GRINSTEAD ⁜

∾ *Snakes and guinea pigs* ∾

Snakes have always been considered an unlucky omen in Sussex, so you can imagine the public outcry in 1936 when a statue depicting the serpent and staff of Asclepius, the Greek god of medicine, was erected on the top of Queen Victoria Hospital. After all, 'It is our hospital,' protested the residents, 'and we should have a say in the matter.' The decision to top the hospital's tower with a bronze serpent apparently aroused suspicion when various mishaps, including the sudden illness of the hospital's matron, hit the hospital. The strength of feeling for such a bad luck symbol was so strong that Sir Robert Kindersley, president of the Hospital Board, agreed to have it taken down and replaced with a crowing rooster weather vane, but when told it would cost £63 to have the serpent moved, the protesters relented and the serpent stayed. Despite the snake omens, the hospital ended up becoming a fortunate place of mutual support for the airmen who fought in the Second World War, who underwent experimental plastic surgery, or facial reconstruction. In June 1941, providing they had gone through at least two surgical procedures, they were entitled to join the elite Guinea Pig Club, named after the rodent then being used in laboratory experiments. The story begins in 1930 when New Zealand surgeon Archibald McIndoe moved from the Mayo Clinic in America to find work in London, but unable to locate anything suitable, his cousin Sir Harold Gillies, an otolaryngologist specialising in plastic surgery, invited him to join his private practice, and offered him a post at St Bartholomew's Hospital. Here he became clinical assistant before being appointed in 1938 to the Royal Air Force as a plastic surgeon. In 1939 he moved to the recently rebuilt Queen Victoria Hospital and founded a centre for plastic and jaw surgery. Less than ten years later he was knighted in recognition of his pioneering plastic surgery techniques and holistic approach to the treatment of Allied aircrew. These young men, who'd became known as the Guinea Pigs, had been badly burned or crushed in their aeroplanes. McIndoe liked to call them the 'boys', which many of them were, the most famous being Richard Hillary, Geoffrey Page, Jimmy Edwards and Bill Foxley. Some endured over thirty painful operations, but the surgeon's biggest enemy was graft rejection. McIndoe had learnt the art of tube pedicle techniques from Sir Harold, and went on to refine a far more effective method of hand and face reconstruction, and the 'walking stalk' skin graft, where a flap of skin, usually from the leg or chest, was stitched into a tube, allowing the surgeon, over a period of weeks, to detach one end of the tube and 'walk' it up the body to the site of the injury. These pedicles were used to recreate airmen's noses, foreheads, lips and chins. Although McIndoe was a brilliant surgeon, he also recognised the importance of rehabilitation and reintegration in society. His patients were allowed to wear their uniforms rather than the 'convalescent blues' of the day, and even barrels of beer were available on the wards to encourage a happy social atmosphere. He felt the 'boys' needed to be prepared for life outside and knew the community would find it difficult to accept their appearance, despite them being heroes. He enlisted the help of two friends, Neville and Elaine Blond, and soon found the locals, in true Sussex style, not only supported his patients but welcomed them into their homes for a meal, earning for East Grinstead the title 'the town that did not stare'. McIndoe encouraged his patients to go out as much as possible and they became a regular sight in the local shops and pubs. The Guinea Pig Club was formed with thirty-nine patients, and by the end of the war they totalled 649. They even had their own club anthem, adapted from the First World World War song *Fred Karno's Army*, which begins:

We are McIndoe's army,
We are his guinea pigs.
With dermatomes and pedicles,
Glass eyes, false teeth and wigs.
And when we get our discharge
We'll shout with all our might:
'*Per ardua ad astra*'
We'd rather drink than fight.

John Hunter runs the gas works,
Ross Tilley wields the knife.
And if they are not careful
They'll have your flaming life.
So, guinea pigs, stand ready
For all your surgeon's calls:
And if their hands aren't steady
They'll whip off both your ears.

The Serpent, the symbol of Asclepius, Greek god of healing and medicine, on the tower of the Queen Victoria Hospital (Conrad Hughes)

We've had some mad Australians,
Some French, some Czechs, some Poles.
We've even had some Yankees,
God bless their precious souls.
While as for the Canadians –
Ah! That's a different thing.
They couldn't stand our accent
And built a separate wing.

The club continued for sixty years, offering practical support, but because of the frailty of the surviving members, ranging in age from 82 to 102, the decision was taken at the 2007 annual meeting to wind down the club, as only seventeen members were still alive. After the war, McIndoe received many awards for his work and was awarded a CBE and knighted in 1947. Two years later he became a member of the council of the Royal College of Surgeons and founded BAPS (British Association of Plastic Surgeons). At just 59 in 1960 he died in his sleep of a heart attack and had the unique honour of his ashes being buried at the Royal Air Force church of St Clement Danes. His legacy lives on and the hospital remains the regional centre for specialist plastic and reconstructive surgery and rehabilitation, with the modern-day burns unit continuing to develop pioneering techniques.

❧ EAST PRESTON ❧

∾ *Built to make amends* ∾

The foundation stone of the first Sunday school, later to become the village school, was laid in 1840, and I expect many of the villagers felt that at last some justice had been achieved. East Preston was a typical farming community with such delightful farm names such as Beehive, Wistaria, Boxtree, Old Yews and Baytree, conjuring up idyllic scenes. But in 1830 these weren't peaceful times, with the agricultural revolution in full swing, especially the enclosure of land and the shift from open field villages to tenant farmers upsetting the farming community. Labourers were now paid by the day or by results, or for short periods like harvesting, hedging, threshing etc. We can imagine how the labourers living at Jasmine, Apple Tree and Baytree cottages in the village must have felt. Little wonder they joined in the Swing Riots spreading across the South and East. They demanded higher wages and the destruction of the threshing machines that were threatening to destroy their winter livelihood, protesting in the only way they knew, by burning hay-ricks. The Ollivers were a large local farming family who owned the whole of nearby West Kingston until 1786, when it was split between two cousins. Samuel Henty took East Kingston and George Olliver West Kingston. Our tale concerns George Olliver and local lad Edmund Bushby, who was born in 1804. George's father William lived at Baytree Cottage with his family, and his brother William lived at Sea Cottage with his young family. Edmund lodged at Two Acres, tenanted by James and Mary Burcher. The year before our story begins had been a wet summer resulting in a poor harvest with only a few dry days in June and September. Snow had fallen in early October before the harvest had been fully gathered, and there was a lot of unrest as workers felt they couldn't face the prospect of another cold and hungry winter. To make matters worse, on 23 November the *London Gazette* published a Home Office notice highlighting rewards of a maximum of £500 for the apprehension and conviction of rioters and arsonists. With winter fast approaching the answer was to thresh by hand, but even an expert at his job could manage only three-quarters of the work in a day. Olliver recognised the problem and on 24 November sent for Edmund Bushby, offering him a flat rate of four shillings a quarter, which Olliver felt was a fair rate for a single person. Bushby was furious and demanded the 'swing' rate of fourteen shillings a week, but Olliver was adamant, and said he'd use his threshing machine instead. After Sunday afternoon service in East Preston church, Olliver was walking home when Edmund overtook him on the footpath and the two started to argue, ending with Olliver saying he'd not employ him. Bushby replied, 'If I can't work by day, then I'll work by night,' a clear reference to poaching or smuggling. That evening Edmund went to Elizabeth Corney's beer shop in the village with his father and brother, and no doubt the topics of conversation were the week's events and how Olliver's machine was depriving them of a livelihood. On the walk home Edmund knew he had to take action, and passing his lodgings borrowed a tinder box and matches from Mary, his landlady at Two Acres. Fifteen minutes later Olliver's hay-rick was well alight, and the alarm was raised. As the flames were being doused the brothers were heard to say, 'Let it burn,' and wished Olliver was in the middle of it. Olliver reported it, and Bushby was arrested and taken to Horsham Gaol where he spent three weeks locked in a cell with other prisoners before being taken to Lewes Assizes. His trial began on 21 December, and as there was little evidence except for Mary's story, Edmund should have been given a lesser sentence, but in his summing up the judge admitted that although the offence warranted punishment by death, it was seldom carried out, but in this case someone must be made an example of. On Christmas Day Edmund and another arsonist, 18-year-old Thomas Goodman, accused of burning a barn in Battle, were taken back to Horsham Gaol, where Edmund made a full confession of the crime to the chaplain and to George Olliver, but to no avail. Later that week his brothers and sisters visited him, and on New Year's Day Edmund climbed the steps to the scaffold. The chaplain read the Lord's Prayer, and a crowd of some 800 to 900 watched as the bolt was drawn. Edmund's body was taken down and given to his brothers, placed in a cart and taken back to East Preston, where three days later he was laid to rest in an unmarked grave in the churchyard, as is recorded in the parish registers. Thomas Goodman was to follow Edmund to the scaffold, but at the last minute was reprieved and transported to the penal colony in Tasmania. A few months later George Olliver received his reward of £500 from the Treasury, the maximum paid for the successful prosecution of an arsonist. However, the villagers never forgave him, although he didn't use the reward for himself, but covered the expenses of the prosecution, and the Bushby family's visits to Lewes and Horsham before the execution. Olliver also offered Edmund's father £200 compensation, but he refused it.

Another story claims that Edmund's brother William was the arsonist, but as he was married with young children, Edmund took the blame. Perhaps as a final act of remorse Olliver used the money to found a charity that eight years later built the first village Sunday school that eventually became the village school, and remained so until 1951 when Lashmar Road School opened. Interestingly, the position chosen for the school was next to the labourer's allotment gardens and the foundation stone faced the cottage occupied by Edmund's father. Was this George Olliver's silent memorial to the man he betrayed and who was so harshly dealt with? Over the years Edmund Bushby became a martyr for victimisation, his story touching the heartstrings of many farm labourers in the county.

⚜ EBERNOE ⚜

∾ *Horn Fair* ∾

On St James's Day, 25 July, the tiny hamlet of Ebernoe comes alive when they hold their curious annual Cricket Match and Horn Fair. The ancient custom was revived in 1864 after a long lapse, and the main activity of the day, a cricket match, is played between the village and a neighbouring team. The batsman who scores the most runs on the winning side is presented with a shield with horns of a ram mounted on it. The ram is usually prepared for roasting around 8.30 that morning, and as the match proceeds, the sheep cooks. During the interval for lunch the sheep is paraded to the pavilion, and the Horn Fair song is sung before the meat is shared out. The song was not written especially for Ebernoe but it appears to have been used in Kent since at least the nineteenth century and has been adapted.

Ebernoe Horn Fair 2007 (Wiki Commons)

As I was a-walking one fine summer morn,
So soft was the wind and the waves on the corn.
I met a pretty damsel upon a grey mare,
And she was a-riding upon a grey mare.
'Now take me up behind you, fair maid, for to ride,'
'Oh no, and then Oh no, for my mammy she would chide,
And then my dear old daddy would beat me full sore,
And never let me ride on his grey mare no more.
If you would see Horn Fair you must walk on your way.
I will not let you ride on my grey mare today.
You'd rumple all my muslin and uncurl my hair,
And leave me all distrest to be seen at Horn Fair.'
'O fairest of damsels, how can you say no?
With you I do intend to Horn Fair for to go.
We'll join the best of company when we do get there,
With horns on their heads, boys, the finest at the Fair.'

⁂ FAIRWARP ⁂

∞ *Life on the open road* ∞

Buried here is one of the great characters of yesteryear. Everyone in the surrounding villages knew Edwin Russell, who led a wandering life, carrying all his possessions around in a large kettle. He was harmless, if a little eccentric, and belonged to a well-off family, but they disowned him. He was brought up by his grandmother, and one Sunday she asked him to look after dinner as it cooked while she went to church. Edwin must have decided that the dinner needed an extra ingredient, and slipped his grandmother's kitten alive into the pot. When she returned, furious, she threw him out. He spent the rest of his life wandering around the villages surrounding Ashdown Forest, and slept wherever he could. Once he found a warm pigsty to sleep in, and made it home, but it became so filthy, the farmer turned him out. On another occasion he used an old wheelbarrow, housed in an open-sided barn, as a bed. Every evening he'd sing, accompanied

by his old battered tuneless accordion, keeping everyone awake, and was forced to move on. He'd wear a top hat, trimmed with feathers or decorated in coloured paper, and he loved anything glittering or bright; if anyone gave him a coloured decoration he'd finger it with delight. He also wore a collection of medals stuck to his coat, but most of all he enjoyed taking all his clothes off

Edwin Russell, the man who loved to take all his clothes off and walking around naked, balancing them on his head. Not surprisingly no-one invited him into their homes, but the villagers were always kind to him, and only too willing to give him food to eat or boil a kettle for him to have a wash or make a hot drink. One extremely cold winter in the 1890s he lost several toes to frostbite and well-wishers took pity on him, making certain that he had a comfortable bed in Uckfield Workhouse Infirmary, which he called 'the fatting coop'. Once the warmer weather came Edwin discharged himself and resumed his nomadic lifestyle, and despite his harsh outdoor life he was well over 70 when he died.

✢ FERRING ✢

∽ *Honest miller or cunning smuggler?* ∽

The eighteenth-century miller and poet John Olliver was an eccentric character who delighted in surrounding himself in mystery. He was reputed to have been a smuggler and used his mill for signalling the all-clear to ships arriving with illicit goods. In 1765 at the age of 50, he began building his own tomb on land owned by William Westbrooke Richardson on Highdown Hill, which had once been the site of an Iron Age camp, a Saxon burial cemetery and a Roman bath house. Olliver visited the tomb every day and sat meditating with his bible on his knees. The inscription on the tomb lid dated 1766 confirms it was built twenty-seven years before he died, and legend informs us that if you run around his tomb twelve times at midnight, his ghost will jump out of it and chase you. The tomb is elaborately engraved with many verses, although most are now very worn and unreadable. One of the verses he penned is as follows:

> My tomb on a lofty hill doth stand,
> Where I sit and view both sea and land;
> With iron palisades I am surrounded in,
> The expense of it I value not a pin.
> For in my own works I take great delight,
> And praise my MAKER day and night;
> When death doth call then I must go
> With him whether I would or no,
> And leave my mill and all behind,
> In hopes a better place to find.

Like others, John Olliver is said to be buried upside down because he believed that at the Last Judgement the world would turn 'topsy-turvy', and he wanted to be the first to be facing the right way up. He was born in Lancing in 1709 and worked the old mill there before taking over his father's mill in 1750. Before the tomb was complete he kept a coffin under his bed, so it was available if needed, and inscribed on it are the following words:

> Beneath my bed my coffin stands,
> On four wheels swift it runs.
> I am always proud to show the same,
> And why, my neighbours, do you me blame.

Some claimed the coffin was used as a hiding place for his smuggled goods, and his spacious tomb to store more contraband. Others claim the verses inscribed around the tomb are merely elaborate codes revealing where the miller hid the proceeds of his illegal activities. When he died his wife established a tea chalet near the tomb that became popular with visitors to Worthing, but sadly in November 1982 vandals badly damaged the tomb and destroyed many of the inscriptions. Oddly there is no burial entry in the register for John Olliver, but on 26 January 1812 there is a footnote which reads: 'John Olliver of this Parish, Miller, was buried under the Tomb on High Down Hill, April 26 1793, aged 83.' As you'd imagine his funeral drew a crowd of thousands, as his body in its white painted coffin was

Miller's tomb or a store for contraband? (Conrad Hughes)

brought from his house by young maidens all dressed in white and carried around the field. The sermon, read by his granddaughter Ann Street, was claimed to have been written by John, but it was actually taken from a printed volume of sermons written by the Church of England clergy. A more recent haunting appears to have occurred in July 1983 and was reported in the *Worthing Gazette and Herald* on 29 July. Two schoolboys from Durrington High School reported that whilst camping on Highdown Hill and, having heard the story about running around the tomb twelve times, set their alarms, and at midnight actually ran around the tomb. Nothing happened, but as they were walking away they heard footsteps and turned to see the ghost of John Olliver. One of the boys was only ten yards away and said, 'He was a very old man with a pale face, and I think he had a moustache. He was losing his hair and was very short.' Whatever the truth we will never know, but the hill continues to be a favourite spot for dog walkers, family picnickers, and so the tales of John Olliver will live on.

⁕ FOREST ROW ⁕

∾ *Not the infamous mail train robbery* ∾

It was late on Monday 27 June 1801 when the main coach carrying post, cash and a few paying passengers from Brighton to East Grinstead made its scheduled stop at the Chequers Posting Inn to pick up more mail, before making its slow climb up Wall Hill. Although these were dangerous times, the occupants felt safe under the protection of an armed Post Office guard wearing his distinctive scarlet and gold livery, but at the foot of the hill by the entrance to the old Roman road, 70-year-old John Beaston and 27-year-old William Whalley Beaston, his adopted son, were hiding in wait. John Beaston, a native of Edinburgh, had retired after a life at sea to keep a respectable inn in the town, but when William took it over a series of misfortunes forced him to move to London and set up another business that ended in bankruptcy. William fled to Hartfield, but on a visit to London he met up with John, now unemployed. The conversation turned to money, and together they planned to give themselves enough financial security for the rest of their lives, relying on William's experiences of the Sussex area. On the Saturday the pair travelled as far as the Rose and Crown Inn, Godstone, where they stayed overnight before continuing to Wall Hill the following day. As the coach approached under the charge of William Edwards, one of the Beastons stopped the horse whilst the other pointed a pistol at the post boy, telling him he wouldn't be harmed if he kept quiet and obeyed orders. The pair led the horse and coach into a field, ransacked the mail, and fled back to Hartfield with £4,000 or £5,000, a vast sum of money in those days. They thought they had got away with it, but later were caught in Liverpool and taken first to Bow Street in London, then to the County Gaol

The mail coach left Chequer's Inn only to be ambushed by the Beastons (Conrad Hughes)

in Horsham. At their trial at the Sussex Assizes on 29 March 1802, Judge Baron Hotham found both guilty and sentenced them to be hanged at the spot where their crime was committed. They travelled by cart from Horsham, seated on their own coffins, and their hangings were the last of highwaymen and amongst the last public hangings in England. The gallows were erected and on 7 April 1802 some 3,000 people turned up to watch their gruesome end. Even today Forest Row is still only a small town, so the number proved people were prepared to travel to see a hanging.

∾ *Memorial to a grandson* ∾

The present village hall, a gift from the Freshfield family of Kidbrooke Park, is distinctive in having an almost Germanic look to it, and replaced the first hall built in memory of 14-year-old Henry Douglas, son of alpine mountaineer Douglas William Freshfield and his wife. It was officially opened on 4 November 1892 by the Hon. A.E. Gathorne Hardy MP on a site that had been in the possession of the owners of Kidbrooke Park for many years, possibly bought from the Abergavanny family in 1874. Like Henry's life, the hall's was short, as it burnt down, leaving only the shell of the front of the building, in February 1895, the day after Henry's grandfather Douglas Ray was buried. It was a particularly bitterly cold day, and Mrs Crittle and another village woman were busy preparing vegetables for the soup kitchen provided for the poor by the Freshfield family, when suddenly the door burst open and Mrs May, the caretaker's wife, shouted that her apartment was on fire. She is also reputed to have said earlier that when Mr Freshfield died, the place 'would never be any good.' The Forest Row fire brigade tried to put out the blaze but were hampered by their poor equipment; the only water available was from the little pond on the green and that froze in the hoses and burst them. East Grinstead fire brigade was called to help, and with longer hoses and water from the Medway they were able to bring the fire under control. The hall was rebuilt to keep alive the memory of the original founder and to be used by all parishioners. Over its long history since reopening on 17 November 1895, it has seen many milestones. Before the fire the first hall was used for a meeting on 12 June 1894 to explain the new Local Government Act which created Forest Row parish. In the same year a working men's club was formed, and from December 1895 mothers' meetings were held weekly. Today the hall has its management committee and remains a fitting memorial to a family that did so much for the community long before the days of care in the community.

The Germanic-looking Forest Row village hall, built by the Freshfield family (Conrad Hughes)

❖ FULKING ❖

∾ *He taught the blind to read* ∾

Louis Pasteur said 'Chance favours the prepared mind', and this is certainly true of William Moon who, together with his devoted wife and children, created, developed and promoted a system for teaching blind people to read. As the result of scarlet fever, 4-year-old William lost the sight in one eye, leaving the other severely impaired, and although fate may not have dealt him a good hand, he turned his adversity into a success story that helped so many visually impaired people. As a child he found it easier to write on a slate with chalk, because reading ordinary print was difficult unless there was a good contrast between the paper and print. Although born in Horsmonden in the neighbouring county, he was descended from an old Rotherfield family. When his parents moved to Brighton William continued to live in Kent with his grandparents. His father died when he was 7, and William was educated at a London school for sighted children, and he always believed that blind students should be allowed to learn alongside sighted peers. Today this is encouraged, but in the early 1800s was unusual. During his time at school he underwent a series of surgical operations, but without modern technology none was successful. At 18 he left school, and joined his widowed mother and sister in Brighton where he studied to become a minister, but his hopes were dashed when in 1840, aged 21, he became totally blind. Just before losing his sight completely William was returning to Brighton via the Lewes Road when his sight suddenly failed. A farm cart happened to pass and he walked behind it following the sound of the horse's hooves until he reached the outskirts of the town and arrived home safely. For a while his sight fluctuated; his sister Mary was always willing to help her brother, but I don't expect he was popular when, thirsty for information, he would go into Mary's room at night, light a candle and ask her to read to him. Unable to see to study, he tried various embossed types to teach other blind people to read, and formed a day school with several blind and some deaf and dumb pupils, but after a few years decided that the system was too complicated for most, and decided to create one of his own. William developed a keen sense of hearing and became attracted to the sweet voice of a lady at the Methodist meetings in the town. She was Miss Mary Ann Claudle, daughter of a Brighton surgeon, who one day when his sister did not arrive to take him home from the meeting, stepped forward and offered to help. A friendship soon blossomed and within a week or two William asked her to marry him; six weeks later they married. The couple encountered financial difficulties from the outset; Mary attempted to run an embroidery shop, and they were constantly moving from one lodging house to another. Despite the various moves William obtained a wooden printing press and began to print passages of scripture using his simple embossed lettering. They had two children: Robert who went on to became a physician in Philadelphia, and Adelaide, born a year after Robert, who became her father's lifelong companion. Mary died in 1864, and two years later William married Anna Maria Elsade, granddaughter of William Leeves, composer of *Auld Robin Gray*. Meanwhile, in France 24-year-old Louis Braille had invented an alphabet using a more complex military system of dots to allow soldiers to read in the dark, and although it became the standard alphabet after his death, it was little known outside Paris. William based his system on the standard alphabet and chose characters that were either unaltered or modified forms of the Roman alphabet, comprising raised shapes to help blind people of any age to read by touch. As the characters were large and over half the letters bore a strong resemblance to the print equivalent, it was particularly suitable for people who lost their sight in later life, or had a limited sense of touch. Compared to Braille, William's system had two disadvantages: texts were bulky – in fact the Bible ran to 4,000 pages in fifty-eight volumes; and it was laboriously slow to produce. Although it is not often used today, it was very successful in the nineteenth century, and William received several awards during his lifetime. He was elected to the Royal Geographical Society in 1852, the Royal Society of Arts in 1857, and awarded an honorary degree by the University of Philadelphia in 1871. Two years later, in 1873, he published *Light for the Blind, A History of the Origin and Success of Moon's system of Reading for the Blind* and was instrumental in founding and promoting local Home Teaching Societies and their free lending library of embossed books. Soon his type was adapted into other languages in many parts of the world, the first, made as an experiment, in Irish. The next language tackled was Chinese, because William knew how prevalent blindness was in China, and longed to provide reading material for them. One day a dear friend, a sea captain, called on William. 'So Dr Moon I hear you can't leave the Chinese alone now.' William replied, 'Not all the time they have any blind among them.' William also met a young blind girl who thought horses stood upright and walked on two legs, and so embossed 'pictures for the blind' were devised to show common objects by touch.

In 1890 William had the Croft built at Fulking as a family summer retreat, replacing an earlier one on the same site. It sits well back from the road and is a rather grand substantial house. Two years later in the autumn, William had a slight stroke and spent the winter months in Brighton, returning the following year to the Croft, but his health was poor. In order to help him take regular exercise Adelaide had a path laid around the lawn with a railing for support so he could take a walk any time. He was always eager to hear reports from his daughter, who played a major role in the success of Moon, and helped run the press at Queen's Road, Brighton. Just before he died suddenly on 10 October 1894, a Brighton friend called on him and he said, 'It has been for me a long night, but a bright day.

The Croft at Fulking, the Moon family summer residence

God has been pleased to give me the talent of blindness and I have tried to do my best to use it.' William's funeral was attended by many of his blind pupils who sang around his grave as his body was interred in the Brighton cemetery. Ten years after his death, Adelaide died, but some years before he died, he'd signed over the freehold to his premises, so that the printing of embossed books could continue.

⚜ GUESTLING ⚜

∾ *A sad victim of circumstance* ∾

Mary Ann Plumb, like many women in Victorian times, put up with her lot, seeing no way out, until she set about destroying herself and her family, and almost succeeded. In prison she wrote a letter for her remaining children summing up her miserable existence.

Forty long years did I live and did not think I had a God nor a soul to save, and now my sins have found me out. I have not said much when I have been told, for I was ashamed of my sinful state before God and man. If I had never been brought to Lewes prison I have done plenty to deserve a worse death than mine. I do pray to be forgiven by God and man through the blood of Him that died upon the cross, and if God be merciful to me I think I shall be the biggest sinner that ever was pardoned.

Mary was the eldest of five children born into a poor hardworking rural family and received a simple education at the local school, although deemed to be a lazy, devious child. One day, as she was their housekeeper, she was left in the house alone while her parents worked in the fields. They returned to find several articles of clothing missing, and Mary Ann denied all knowledge of their whereabouts, but it transpired she had pawned them. She was sent into service as a maid, but was more interested in flirting with a farmhand, Richard Geering, than working, and when it was discovered she was pregnant she was sent home in disgrace. Her parents were horrified. They had a good reputation in the community as an upright family, and didn't want the shame of having an unmarried daughter to cope with. They insisted she married Richard, but she was equally insistent that she didn't love him, but after much pressure reluctantly married at Westfield church, near the family home. Three months later Mary Ann's first child was born and they moved to Harmer's Cottages near Guestling, where Richard found work as a labourer for Mr John Veness. Richard had a quick and violent temper, and with Mary Ann's explosive temperament, it was not a happy relationship, but despite frequent quarrels they managed to produce eight children. Mary Ann became a devoted mother, and although she rarely took them to church, she taught them to pray, and herself to read and write by copying from the children's school books. Her relationship with Richard was one of constant arguments and unhappy tolerance. He considered her extravagant with money, she accused him of being tight-fisted, and it soon became a habit for her to travel to Hastings on a Monday morning, pawning the family's Sunday best, returning to redeem it on Saturday so they could wear it on Sunday. Despite being poor, all those employed paid weekly into the Guestling Friendly Society, entitling each member of the family to a payment of eightpence a day during illness, and all funeral expenses in the event of death. In times of no state benefit this was essential in order for a family to survive. When Mary Ann was 48 years old, her eldest son William's wife died of consumption leaving three small children, and he agreed to move in with his parents and pay 9s a week for board and lodgings. However, it turned out to be less than ideal, as Mary Ann's younger boys were jealous of her taking on the role of mother to the little ones. In revenge her own children began to take Richard's side in quarrels, making life even more difficult. No doubt she felt isolated and sought solace by becoming a regular church-goer. One day three words in a sermon *a murdering mother*, reverberated around her mind, plaguing her by day and giving her strange dreams at night. Two years earlier Richard had inherited a sum of £20 and placed it in a savings bank in Hastings, giving the book to his sister for safekeeping. At the time they were in in arrears on their rent, and Mary Ann thought the money should have been used to clear their debts rather than banked. In March the following year Richard asked his sister to withdraw £5 for him and keep the book. Mary Ann was furious and a few months later she asked her sister-in-law for the book saying that Albion, her son, had asked to see it. The sister handed the book over, but didn't tell her brother. Mary Ann went straight to the bank and withdrew most of it, leaving just 1s 4d in the account. In September 1848 the couple had yet another row about rent arrears. Richard was now working as a labourer on Mr Arkoll's farm, and one day he and fellow worker William Apps were ordered to collect oats. At midday both men sat under a hedge to eat their lunch and share some home-brewed beer supplied by the master. Each worker was given a horn holding about half a pint of beer, which they usually gulped down in one swallow, but Richard had great difficulty, and only managed to drink half his quota. Later that afternoon he was violently sick, but continued to work until around 7 p.m. The next two days he appeared to be fine and went to work as usual, but on the Saturday Apps called for Richard, and was told by Mary Ann that he'd been sick for most of the night and wouldn't be going to work. After his shift Apps called back and was informed that Richard was no better. The next day Mr Pocock, a local surgeon, was called and medication prescribed, but when he returned to see how his patient was progressing, he found Richard dead, and based on what Mary Ann said issued a certificate that Richard had died from heart disease. That same day Mary Ann applied to the Friendly Society and received £4 18s towards the cost of the funeral, and a further sum of 3s 4d for the days he was ill. Fifteen weeks after his father's death, Mary Ann's son George, aged 21, became ill and when Judith Veness called, Mary Ann told her George was suffering from the same heart condition as his father. For several weeks he was nursed by his mother by day and his brother James at night, sometimes feeling better, but always complaining of a raging thirst with violent bouts of vomiting. Mr Pocock prescribed doses of castor oil, but George grew worse and died. Mary Ann sent for Mrs Veness and asked her to prepare the body for the coffin. She was surprised to find the body on the bed dressed in a blue-striped cotton shirt and stockings instead of the usual shroud. Mary Ann claimed it was her son's wish. Mrs Veness, disgusted there was no shroud, suggested a piece of calico should at least be placed over the body, and his mother agreed. Six weeks after George's funeral, financed by the Guestling Friendly Society, 26-year-old James became ill with symptoms resembling those of his father and brother. James told Mr Pocock that he had a 'heat in the heart', and on 6 March he died. Three weeks later on Good Friday, 18-year-old Ben became ill after drinking tea, and on Easter Sunday after drinking tea for breakfast he was violently sick, but managed to go to the farm to feed the animals. Mary Ann confided in Mr Foster, a neighbour, that she was worried about Ben as she had been told by a fortune-teller that she would lose her husband and a number of her children before three years were out. For two days Ben complained of a 'heat in his inside', then made a slight recovery before slipping into a relapse after a drink with his dinner. Three days later Mary Ann called Mr Pocock, then Mr Ticehurst, a medical attendant, was called, and suspecting that Ben was being poisoned, removed him from the cottage. Mr Ticehurst contacted the coroner and the bodies of Richard and his sons were exhumed and tested. Mary Ann was suspected of administering poison and was taken to Hastings, whilst her three youngest children were taken into a poorhouse. The inquest was held at the White Hart at Guestling, and evidence was given that Mary Ann had, on various occasions, bought packets of arsenic from a Hastings chemist. Medical evidence showed that Richard and James had arsenic in their bodies, and James mercury. Although she pleaded not guilty to three charges of murder and one of an attempt on the life of Ben, she was committed for trial on 7 August 1849, and the case became known as the Guestling Murderess. The sad marriage was examined in fine detail, and the witness for the Crown, Mr Hunt, did his best in her defence, stating that the arsenic found in the body of George and Richard could easily have been taken by mistake. As for the money received from the Friendly Society, he said it was certainly not enough to murder for. Mary Ann, he said, was a kind and affectionate mother, and although there was much quarrelling it couldn't have been a motive. His arguments had no effect and Mary Ann was sentenced to hang. Only eleven days after sentence a huge crowd began to assemble on both sides of North and Little East Streets,

The White Hart at Guestling where the inquest took place (Conrad Hughes)

Lewes. Thousands of people gathered on the slopes of Cliffe Hill and police were stationed at every corner in case of trouble. The lower windows of the houses opposite the prison were barricaded, but the upper floors filled with spectators. All morning there was a buzz of excitement and as midday approached the prisoner appeared, dressed all in black, bareheaded and with a black shawl with a multi-coloured border pinned around her neck, supported by two turnkeys. She mounted the steps and stood as the clergyman said prayers, then the executioner stepped forward, placed a cap over her head and fixed the cord around her neck, passing it over the cross beam. Her hands were not tied and the crowd saw they were clasped in prayer. Finally she was at peace, her tragic life over. Before her execution she made a full confession to the chaplain who believed she was truly sorry, and claimed she didn't murder for money, but to put an end to her misery. She told the chaplain she had contemplated suicide in prison but reading her bible she came across these words: *He that endureth to the end shall be saved, and so may be I.*

H

⁘ HAILSHAM ⁘

∞ *The Great Omi* ∞

It may be popular to have a tattoo on your body today, but the idea is certainly not new. Julius Caesar wrote that all Britons stained their skins with woad, and when Ötzi, the iceman, was discovered deep in the Italian Alps in 1991 he had no fewer than sixty-one tattoos on his body, proving they were used some 5,000 years ago. Horace Ridler went one step further, and although his last recorded words were, 'underneath it all I'm just an ordinary man', there was nothing average about him. His body was covered in swirling blue-black markings, his lower teeth filed to fit into the top teeth like fangs, and through his ears were ivory daggers on which hung large ivory rings. His fingernails were sharpened to a point and painted bright red, and a tusk inserted through his nose completed the look, turning him into a circus sensation and one of the highest performers of his day. He was born in 1892 into an extremely wealthy Surrey family who had several properties and a well-stocked stable of horses. Horace was passionate about horses and the family groom, Joe Green, taught him how to become a competent rider. Joe was once a circus clown and young Horace would listen, fascinated by his tales of circus life and skills of showmanship. Horace enjoyed all the comforts and security that money could buy, and after leaving school joined the army as a commissioned officer, but before he took up his post his father gave him a generous allowance to enable him to tour Europe and North Africa. Wherever he went he was attracted to the music halls, and spent days enjoying the circus acts, as well as jugglers and snake charmers. Tour over, he took up his commission as a second lieutenant, and soon after his father died, leaving him a substantial inheritance that he squandered on wild parties, gambling and poor investments. Suddenly he found he couldn't live the life expected of an officer and he resigned. Having no skills at his fingertips he tried many jobs, then the First World War broke out and he re-enlisted as a cavalry trooper and was decorated for bravery. He rose through the ranks to major before retiring with a small pension but few job prospects. He invested his modest savings in a chicken farm but could not manage money and lost everything. He turned to bareback horse riding, and although he was good, there were others far better.

He also found that after being part of rigid army life, he wanted to be different, to stand out from the norm. He thought back to his travels, and how there was always work for the oddities in life. Why not become a show attraction, covering myself in tattoos from head to toe, he thought. The first tattooist chosen claimed to be Chinese, and after some crude unskilled tattoos on his arms, he was able to make a modest living working in music halls and fairgrounds. He realised that if he were to make any money at all, he would need to give his audience more, and this included tattooing his face. Several tattooists were reluctant to work on the face, and he nearly gave up, until he discovered Brighton-born George Burchell working in London, but he too refused the commission, saying the dyes were indelible and Horace would have to spend the rest of life with his new image. More importantly he would probably lose friends and family because of his appearance. But Horace was adamant. He knew what he wanted. Horace had married Gladys, an attractive lady who backed him, so on his return with a letter confirming his wish to be tattooed, approved and signed by his wife, Burchell had no option, and tattooing began in two-hour sessions, three times a week. One hundred and fifty hours later the image was complete, although tattooing in those days had its dangers and Horace was forced to spend hours in bed waiting for swellings to subside and coping with the ever present risk of infection. Also the black dye used changed to cobalt blue on the skin, and it took 15 million needle pricks to cover the face, and 500 million more to cover the body. Thankfully it paid off and shortly after completion he toured the UK with the Bertram Mills Circus, under the stage name of Omi, after reading about Omai, the tattooed man Captain Cook found in 1774. Despite thousands of people wanting to see the world's most tattooed man, he didn't receive any other bookings after that initial success, and was forced to take a tour with a French circus, with disastrous consequences. Deceived by the organisers and billed as a new form of animal-man, they claimed his body markings were natural, and made him perform next to a cage of lions. Matters were made even worse because he spoke no French and the circus troop no English and he even had to pay his own way, so any money he earned went on food and accommodation for him and Gladys. He became ill and his employers had little sympathy, making him work without a break. He stuck it out for three months then quit. One Sunday he took himself off to the local doctor who discovered he was suffering from a form of gas poisoning caused by the urine in the lions' cage. The couple returned to England, and he decided that a more dramatic approach was needed so he had his nose pierced by a vet to enable different ivory tusks to be inserted. His ear lobes were stretched to about the size of a coin and rings inserted. He visited a dentist to have his teeth filed down to sharp points, and brought very colourful clothes and long gold coloured boots. Supported by his wife, things began to take off when they travelled to America, arriving in 1939. Staying at the Hotel Claridge in Times Square, he became an instant attraction, and joined Ripley's *Believe it or Not* shows. Gladys was his constant companion and compère, calling herself Omette, and she even created an explanation for his tattoos, spinning out a tale of how he was captured and tortured by natives in New Guinea. During the Second World War they became the star attraction in Canada, giving shows for war charities and the troops. At this time he began signing his pitch cards as 'the Barbaric Beauty', and wore sequinned gold velvet robes specially woven in the French mills at Lyon. In the middle of the 1950s Omi and Omette retired to a mobile home at Golden Cross Caravan Park near Hailsham, where the couple were regularly seen shopping and going about their everyday life. One local shopkeeper said, 'Horace was a well educated man who acted quite normally and livened up our lives.' Horace died in 1969, aged 77 and Gladys followed him in 1973, and they are both buried in nearby Chalvington churchyard.

A postcard of the Great Omi, before piercing his nose and ears

❖ HAMMERPOT ❖

∞ *A beer that came full circle* ∞

When an unnamed ship was wrecked carrying a mixed cargo including a vast number of bottles of porter, it became known as the Bottle Ship. The wooden merchant ship, carved from oak with possibly three masts, had on board some willow-patterned crockery marked Read and Clementson; that helped date the wreck to within two years, as the markings were only used for a short period between 1833 and 1835. During a dive in 1983, around 500 complete and corked bottles of the typical 'porter' shape in half-pint size, common between 1760 and 1918, were raised from the seabed. Some of the bottle corks were inscribed 'Kinnley Williams of London', but all attempts to locate the brewers failed. The bottles still contained some porter, a very dark ale based on roasted malt of a type popular in the eighteenth century and known as 'working class beer'. From the samples of yeast and the residue preserved in the corked bottles it was possible to recreate the original beer and this was sold as flag porter by the Darwin Brewery in the UK in 1991. Sixteen years later, the local Hammerpot Brewery introduced a Hammerpot Bottle Wreck Porter from September to March, which has become very popular, and is produced in nine-gallon firkins as well as bottles.

The willow-patterned crockery that helped to date the 'Bottle Ship', together with some beer bottles (Conrad Hughes)

A label used on the Sussex ale made by the Hammerpot Brewery (Hammerpot Brewery)

⚜ HARTING ⚜

∞ *The fun-loving country gent* ∞

When the nation, grateful for Wellington's victory at Waterloo, wished to show their gratitude and present him with a country mansion, Uppark was suggested. The Duke of Wellington wrote to its owner, Sir Harry Fetherstonhaugh, on gilt-edged paper saying he was delighted and 'should prefer that place than any other'. He set out to visit on 19 July 1816, but on arriving at Harting was shocked to find a steep road up to the house. Wellington decided he would need to buy horses for his stables every eighteen months or so, and reluctantly turned down the house, which was just as well seeing that Sir Harry had quite a reputation of being a lavish entertainer with an eye for the pretty ladies. In 1780 he brought a beautiful young 15-year-old Cheshire showgirl, Emma Hart, to live at Uppark, hiring her to dance naked on the table to entertain his guests. She lived with him for a year, but he was

Uppark offered to the Duke of Wellington for his victory at Waterloo, and where Emma Hart danced naked on the table (Conrad Hughes)

more interested in drinking and hunting and ignored her. When he discovered that she was pregnant for the second time he was furious and abandoned her, but she soon found solace in another lover. She'd met Charles Grenville at Uppark, but after keeping her for a while he too tired of her, and after the baby was born suggested she went on a trip to Naples. Her host was his ageing uncle Sir William Hamilton, Ambassador to the Kingdom of Naples, but unknown to Emma, she had been exchanged in return for his uncle paying off Grenville's debts. They later married, and seven years later Emma, Lady Hamilton, met Admiral Lord Nelson in Naples and became his mistress. When he died at the Battle of Trafalgar and she was left destitute, Sir Harry Fetherstonhaugh paid off her debts. He remained a bachelor and became something of a recluse in later life, and aged 70 in 1825 he heard 18-year-old dairymaid Mary Ann Bullock singing as she went about her work and proposed to her in the dairy. She was so shocked at his proposal that she was speechless, but Sir Harry told her if the answer was yes, to cut a chunk out of the leg of lamb being served to his table that evening. We assume she recovered from the shock, because the joint arrived at the table with a thick slice cut out of it. Little is known of their relationship, except that he provided her with a governess, educated her as a lady, and sent her, at the age of 21, to Paris to a finishing school. Mary Ann turned out to be a devoted wife for twenty-one years, looking after him until he died at the age of 92.

⚜ HASTINGS ⚜

∾ *Sacrificial offering or witches' familiars?* ∾

When builders were carrying out renovation work on the first-floor chimney of the grade two listed Stag Inn in the 1940s, they were surprised to discover the perfectly preserved bodies of two smoke-blackened mummified cats. The building dates back to the sixteenth century, and they may have been placed there as a sacrifice in an attempt to ward off the plague, and then bricked up by a witch, Hannah Clarke, who is known to have occupied the inn in 1665. Or perhaps the inquisitive cats simply entered the chimney, found they were unable to get down and were overcome by smoke, effectively being smoke-dried which prevented the remains from decaying. From the time they were discovered until the1980s, the cats hung from hooks in the main bar, but were then carefully taken down and placed in a glass-fronted wooden case and hung on the wall above the bar.

∾ *Why should we find a tomb on a wrecked ship?* ∾

The Danish wooden schooner *Thomas Lawrence* sank in 1862 on route to the Danish Virgin Islands, with a tombstone on board intriguingly inscribed in English commemorating a Danish family. It reads 'Here repose the mortal remains of Julia Adriane Jahncke, born Beverboudt in St Croix the 7th February 1827, died in St Thomas 6 March 1858. Franz Friedrich Jahncke, born 6 March 1858, died the 19 March 1858.' The story involves Julia, who died in childbirth at the age of 31, and little Franz who died thirteen days later. Mr Jahncke was about to remarry and wished 'to tidy up his affairs' by sending the tombstone out to the Danish Virgin Islands where his wife and child were buried in an unmarked grave. The *Thomas Lawrence*, built around 1838-39 in Sweden, was ordered by Christian August Broberg, a rich Copenhagen ship owner and coffee trader and was so named because at the time Jens Wolff, a relation of Mrs Broberg, was the Danish Consul in London, and Wolff's English wife Isabella had an affair with the painter Thomas Lawrence after he painted her portrait in 1803. The *Thomas Lawrence* left

Mummified cats at the Stag Inn, Hastings (Conrad Hughes)

The tombstone on board the schooner *Thomas Lawrence* (Conrad Hughes by kind permission of the Shipwreck Heritage Centre, Hastings)

Hamburg in 1862 bound for Haiti with a scheduled stop at Charlotte Amalie on St Thomas in the Danish (now American) Virgin Islands to unload the tombstone, but it was rammed amidships on the port side by German steamer *Die Schwalbe* on 10 March 1862 and sank.

∞ British-born Indian brave ∞

Many little boys once loved to play at being Indians, but one boy took the fascination to its limits. On a tour of England in 1935 Archie Belaney enthralled his audiences with tales of wild Canada, the harsh winters he endured, and the native animals he trapped and killed, concluding with how in the end he devoted his life to conservation, before the word was popular. He looked every inch an authentic Indian, dressed in buckskins and moccasins, with weatherbeaten skin and his long hair braided, but behind the façade there lies a curious tale. Archie Stansfield Belaney was not Indian, but born in St James's Road in 1888. His father, George, was always indulging in wild schemes to make his fame and fortune, but not settling to anything. His second marriage was to Archie's American mother, Katherine Kittie, when she is believed to have been under 20. Shortly after Archie was born George scarpered off to Florida to make his fortune as an orange grower and taxidermist, leaving Archie and his mother behind, but she married again and Archie was left to grow up with his grandmother, his father's mother Juliana Belaney, and two aunts, Ada and Carrie. Like many young children Archie loved the outdoors, learning woodcraft, sleeping outdoors and making bird calls, and from the time he could read about Sitting Bull and the wild west he dreamed of becoming a real Indian one day. He told stories that he was actually half Indian, his mother being an American Indian. He attended the grammar school and would draw native Indians in feathered headdresses in the margins of his books. He also loved playing tricks, and using the knowledge gained at Hastings Grammar School chemistry lessons to make small bombs, which he called 'Belaney Bombs'. His first job as a clerk for a timber company abruptly ended when he lowered fireworks down the chimney of the office, which nearly destroyed the building when they exploded. Naturally he was sacked. Desperate to escape his strait-laced aunts, they gave in to his wish to move to Canada seeking adventure. He sailed from Liverpool to Halifax in 1906, and then travelled to Lake Tamagami in Ontario, lodging with a settler who taught him the art of trapping. Archie was in his element, and living with the Ojibwa Indians on Bear Island he listened to the elders telling their stories about hunting and the young braves. He dropped his native English, learning the language of the Ojibwa Indians, and braided his long hair, and in 1910 married local tribe girl Angele Euana. They had a child together and he seemed to settle down to a life with the tribe, but his constant desire for adventure was strong and in 1912 he told his wife he'd taken a job as a ranger and would be away for some time. For six long years he cut himself off from his roots, trapping in the winter, and working as a ranger during the summer months. He earned himself quite a reputation as a drinker and a man that was handy with a knife, telling elaborate, shocking stories in the evenings. By now the First World War had begun, and in 1915 he joined the Canadian Army as a sharpshooter and went to Flanders as a sniper, but he was wounded in the foot and suffered gas poisoning. He returned to England to convalesce, and soon met up with his friends, including a girl, Florence Holmes, who he fell in love with and married in St Leonards, without telling her he was already married. It ended quickly in divorce and he returned to Canada in 1917. He dyed his brown hair black and darkened his skin with henna, but couldn't do anything about his blue eyes. He was still a prankster, and for Victoria Day in 1923 he organised a 'war party'; playing the role of Indian Chief, he symbolically tied a white prisoner to a pole and told him the wrongs that man had done to the Indians. However, he soon realised that Canada was not the country he left, and with fur prices increasing the area was full of trappers hoping to make a fortune. Grey Owl, as he now called himself, was very concerned that the new breed of hunter cared little about the young pups or the pregnant females. Then two things happened to change his thinking; first he met a beautiful girl called Anahareo, whom he nicknamed Pony. She had the ability to bring out the good side of him, and they married. One day he watched as a mother beaver drowned in one of his traps, leaving behind two little kittens. Grey Owl raised his gun to shoot them; he turned and saw the anguish in Anahareo's eyes and slowly lowered the gun. His wife rushed forward, placed the two little orphans under her shirt, and took them to their home, calling them MacGinnis and MacGinty. When they were old enough, Grey Owl planned to sell the pair of kittens, but one night MacGinnis jumped on to the bed and proceeded to give him a good wash before settling down on his chest for the night. Grey Owl's heart melted. He'd noticed the decline in the number of beavers, and began what he later became best known for – conservation. It was a new concept and Grey Owl was amongst its pioneers, so in the spring when MacGinnis and MacGinty ran away to join their beaver friends they were quickly replaced by Jelly Roll and Rawhide, whose adventures found their way into *Country Life* magazine. Next came Grey Owl's first book, *The Men of the Last Frontier*, published in 1931, and in the same year Grey Owl and Anahareo moved to Lake Ajawaan in Prince Albert National Park, Saskatchewan. By now the Canadian Government had heard of his conservation work and did all they could to help, offering him a position as a naturalist. He started a beaver colony, and a string of films followed. Several British tours were arranged between 1935 and 1937, and a visit to Buckingham Palace to meet King George VI and

Grey Owl during a tour to England in 1936, when he met King George VI and the two princesses

the two young princesses. At the end of the tours, Grey Owl returned to Beaver Lodge, but on 10 April 1938 he called the Park Office to say he wasn't feeling well and was taken to Prince Albert Hospital where he fell into a coma and died of pneumonia three days later at just 49. He was buried near his cabin. His first wife Angele, although she had not seen Grey Owl for many years, proved her marriage and inherited most of his estate. Anahareo and Grey Owl had had a daughter Shirley Dawn in 1932, but separated in 1936. She lived to be 80, and when asked how she remembered Grey Owl, she said, 'To me he was an Indian and one of the best men I'd ever met.'

⁕ HEATHFIELD ⁕

For those who could not afford a memorial

Impressed by the advances in his profession as a stone mason, Jonathan Harmer set sail for New York to make a better life for himself and his family, but they soon became distraught when the summer heat and humidity brought swarms of mosquitoes, making it impossible for them to sleep at night. Yellow fever and dysentery had already taken the lives of two of his children, so he returned to England, but whilst on board the same brig that had taken him out to America, he received news that his father had died and was being buried on 1 May 1800. In his will his father bequeathed, 'All such Portland and other stone together with my working Tools and Utensils belonging to the Trade of a stonemason and Bricklayer,

One of Hamer's terracotta headstones

Another of Hamer's terracotta headstones

and Land Surveying Books' to his sons. On his return Jonathan set up business and worked at building up a reputation for quality workmanship. These were hard times and he noticed that many families couldn't afford to commemorate the passing of a loved one with a decent headstone. If they were lucky a good employer or a benefactor contributed to the cost, but these were few and far between. As he carved the headstones for those who could afford them, he began to wonder how he could help those mourning in poverty, and came up with the idea of making a terracotta bas-relief using the same images as those on marble. The mourner could just about pay for the gravestone and have it erected. Some engraved it and then chose a design, and he would make up the bas-relief, to be fixed themselves, or someone paid to fix it at a later date when finances allowed. Jonathan made numerous designs for the recently bereaved to chose from and all were carefully detailed. His work can be seen in numerous churchyards in Sussex as well as this village. There are ornate urns full of flowers and fruit, cherubs for young children's graves and veiled figures and wing feathers, all designed to bring out the natural colours, and available to be ordered in a choice of colour also. Those made of local clay offered a glowing redness, whilst the clay used from further afield produced a pale cream or buff colour. The clay was firmly pressed into the mould, and then using a very sharp tool he worked on the fine details before baking in a wood-fired oven. He died in 1849, no doubt happy to know that he had played a part in helping so many to mourn their much loved relatives.

⁂ HENFIELD ⁑

∞ *Pinch your nose as you look for cats* ∞

Today you don't need to pinch your nose on Pinchnose Green, but I expect you needed to once, because there was a tannery nearby and the process of tanning hides soaked in urine produced a very unpleasant odour. However, you do need to look for cats, and the intriguing tale concerning Cat House, the thatch-roofed house known as The Leeches before it acquired its present name. In the nineteenth century the house belonged to Robert Ward, and legend informs us that a cat belonging to Anglican Canon Nathaniel Woodward killed one of Ward's pet canaries. The two men could never agree on anything, so there was a mutual dislike, and this was the last straw. We can only imagine how Robert, one of a rare breed of true eccentrics, felt when his canary died and he decided to take his revenge. He bought some metal effigies of cats with canaries in their paws, which he positioned around the upper storey of the house, and tied a string through the cats on which hung a large number of bells. As Nathaniel Woodward passed to and from Henfield church, Robert would pull the string, so Nathaniel was greeted with a peal of bells and clanging metal to remind him of his cat's crime. He also arranged a selection of scallop shells, which he would jangle at the same time, and even fired a wooden cannon, much to the annoyance of the neighbours, but eventually Robert was persuaded to control his behaviour.

The Cat House where a cat caught a canary (Conrad Hughes)

❖ ISFIELD ❖

∾ *The White Lady* ∾

In 1915 many men from towns and villages throughout the county were sent to the front line to fight for king and country, leaving behind a sweetheart or a wife. We can all imagine the apprehension running through one local woman's mind as she stands at the end of Platform 1, and kisses her recently wed husband goodbye. No doubt they promise to write, and each eagerly waits for news from the other side of the Channel. One day the lady receives a letter, but it isn't the expected reply to hers, but an official letter informing her that her husband has been killed in action. She is grief-stricken. How is she going to live without him? All day it plays on her mind, and unable to sleep she gets up early, dresses in her white bridal dress and leaves her home. The villagers notice her walking through the village, and think it odd that she's wearing the same white dress she was married in, but purposefully she walks on, acknowledging no-one. She carries on to Isfield station without saying a word to anyone, and walks down Platform 1 to the end, clutching the sides of her dress. She would know the times of the trains and, as the fast train to Brighton approaches the station, she calmly walks straight off the platform on to the tracks in front of the speeding locomotive. She's struck and killed instantly, leaving the station staff devastated. It happened over a hundred years ago, but over the years, on a warm summer's night, her ghost has been seen by many members of staff. The White Lady can be seen walking to the far end of Platform 1 where she stops, looks and slowly walks across the line before disappearing just in front of the signal box where she was killed.

∾ *Molly Mothballs* ∾

Everyone knew of Molly Mothballs, and in these days of state benefits it's hard to believe that well within living memory, home for Molly (or Moggy) was a cave in the rocks at Buckham Hill. Even though the locals christened her with a less than kind name, they were generous to the old lady as she trundled along the lanes pushing an old battered pram. She was given plenty of warm clothes, but never quite understood about changing them, and would pile one layer on top of another until she resembled a small round ball: hence the name. Molly was finally knocked down and killed in an accident involving a military vehicle, and everyone was shocked to learn that she had a small fortune in banknotes carefully sewn inside the linings of her various coats.

⚜ ITCHINGFIELD ⚜

∾ *Whose skull is it?* ∾

Sitting in the churchyard is a rather unusual feature, a detached fifteenth-century priest's house built for the monks sent from Sele Priory in Upper Beeding to collect church tithes. The monk would have ridden through the forest to his destination, but unable to return the same day he would stay in the priest's house overnight taking rest and food, and then celebrate mass the following morning before making his homeward journey. The church itself has an interesting tale to share. The fourteenth-century belfry, which is held together using only wooden

An unusual setting for a priest's house (Conrad Hughes)

pegs and no nails, was being restored in 1865 by Sir Gilbert Scott. When he removed the casing from around one of the old oak roof beams he discovered a human skull, thought to be that of Sir Hector Maclean who fought for the Young Pretender during the Jacobite Rising in 1715. Sir Hector was a friend of the then vicar, Rev. Alexander Hay, who offered him refuge in the church when the rebellion failed, but he was caught and executed for treason. It is also said that during his arrest a bullet was fired in the church and can be seen in one of the oak tower posts. It is thought that the vicar preserved his friend's skull by hiding it in the beams. Interestingly there is an entry in the parish register records that John Maclean was buried there on 28 August 1724. We know that the vicar opened his house to some of his countrymen after the rebellion, but we also know that Rev. Hay died on 30 January 1724, so were Hector and John Maclean related? Could they have been brothers, maybe? As they were living with the Rev. Hay's widow, were they actually related to her? Sadly we have to be content to wonder.

J

⊹ JEVINGTON ⊹

∽ *Jevington Jigg* ∽

No, Jevington Jigg is not a new kind of dance, but the nickname of a well-known organiser of a smuggling gang that operated during the 1780s. James Pettit was also known as Jack Jigg, James or John Pettit, Wilson, Morgan, Gibbs or Williams, whatever name took his fancy. He was the innkeeper of the Eight Bells, a 300-year-old pub, now back under the ownership of the Jevington family. James would offload booty in nearby Birling Gap and Crowlink, and bring the goods up the valley, where he stored it in the cellar of the rectory and the inn. Many of the clergy of the day turned a blind eye for the price of a bottle of brandy or some tobacco, and one story tells of the activities of James coming to the attention of the local authorities. A group of constables were despatched to the inn in the hope of arresting him once and for all, but James was clever. He was playing cards with some friends when someone said that the inn was surrounded by officers. Resourceful as ever, James rushed outside wearing a ladies' bonnet, cloak and petticoat and proceeded to have hysterics, and whilst the constables burst into the inn James made his getaway. His passions were smuggling and horse stealing; he was a sort of Ned Kelly of Sussex. Another story is told of him being arrested together with his friend 'Cream Pot Tom', for stealing a mare in Firle. Tom was hanged, but James was released, leading to rumours that he had betrayed his friend, and he ended up narrowly escaping from the mob who wished to lynch him. One day his luck ran out and he was was finally convicted and deported for fourteen years to Botany Bay, where he probably died.

∽ *The home of Banoffi Pie* ∽

The village is not only famous for smuggling but for the invention, or rather the evolution, of the famous pie by Nigel Mackenzie, owner of the Hungry Monk restaurant, and his chef at the time, Ian Dowling. The story is told on Ian's website (http://iandowding.co.uk/the-completely-true-and-utter-story-of-banoffi-pie/) and begins in the 1960s when the British public were more adventurous about food. Having completed a catering course, Ian's first post was at a small restaurant in Berkshire. The chef prepared the main courses, patés and *patisseries*, and also had a secret recipe which he had brought from America: Blum's Coffee Toffee Pie, which rarely worked as it involved boiling sugar, butter and cream together to produce a thick toffee which was then poured into a pastry case and topped with coffee-flavoured cream. One year later Ian took the post of head chef at the Hungry Monk, taking with him the chef's recipes. They were quietly forgotten, because

The plaque commemorating the birth of Banoffi pie (Conrad Hughes)

he had to do everything as the only chef and the food revolution had begun. As he said, 'There was more to life then than prawn cocktail and steak Diane'. He was encouraged to try out ratatouille, chicken pancakes, and moussaka. During a conversation with his sister, she told him about boiling cans of condensed milk unopened for several hours to make a soft toffee, and he resurrected the Blum's Coffee Toffee recipe. Nigel, the owner, thought Ian could make it even better with a little tweak here and there, and experiments with apples and mandarin oranges were tried before Nigel suggested bananas. Names were needed, but as banana coffee toffee pie was a bit of a mouthful Nigel came up with the word 'Banoffi'. It was meant as a temporary name, but has entered the English language, and Banoffi now has the distinction of being listed in the Oxford English Dictionary, and has even been served at Buckingham Palace and Number Ten. In fact Margaret Thatcher said it was her favourite food to cook. The restaurant has since closed, but a plaque to the birth of Banoffi Pie is attached to the wall.

⊰ KEMPTOWN ⊱

❦ *His beloved Maria* ❦

It was in the spring of 1785 that the twice widowed Maria Fitzherbert was first introduced to George, the Prince Regent, who fell madly in love with her. She was naturally flattered, but not interested. He was so besotted that one day he attempted to stab himself, and drenched in his blood, he sent for her. She agreed provided she was chaperoned by the Duchess of Devonshire, a close friend of the prince. As she approached his bedside, the duchess produced a ring and Maria agreed to take it as a symbol of being pledged to him, then went abroad. Wherever she went the prince wrote to her, and when she returned eighteen months later he pursued her until she finally agreed to marry him, despite being six years older, Roman Catholic, and against the provisions of the Royal Marriages Act of 1772. They went through a form of marriage in secret on 15 December in the drawing room of her house in Park Street, London. The ceremony was performed by one of George's chaplains, the Anglican Rev. Robert Burt whose debts of £500 the prince had paid off so he could be released from Fleet Prison. For nine years Maria was the main woman in his life, but after numerous affairs, one in particularly with Frances, Lady Jersey, the relationship came to an end. Under pressure from Lady Jersey the prince was forced to marry his cousin Caroline of Brunswick, whom he hated; but the marriage meant his mounting debts would be settled and he would acquire an annual income. The prince missed Maria and never entirely abandoned her, continuing to pay her the pension of £3.000 she had received since their marriage. Shortly after his daughter, Princess Charlotte, was born he separated from his wife and begged Maria to return to him, but it took four years to win her back. After being advised by her confessor, who'd received instructions from Rome that she might do so without blame, she returned, and in June 1800 gave a public breakfast to celebrate the occasion. Although they had separate houses they lived together as man and wife, although some say that Maria agreed to return only if the relationship was non-sexual. The prince wanted his lady to have a permanent home near to the Royal Pavilion and commissioned William Porden to design Steine House for her. The prince was always extravagant, and the couple often encountered money problems. On one occasion, returning to Brighton from London, they didn't have enough money between them to pay the post-horses, and were forced to borrow from an old servant, but despite difficulties Maria always said they were the best times of her life. However, the prince was always under the influence of others, and the final straw came around 1811 when a dinner was being given for Louis XVIII at Carlton House. Maria was told she had

Steine House built for Maria Fitzherbert by the Prince Regent (Wiki Commons)

no fixed place at the main table, and must sit according to her rank as plain Mrs Fitzherbert. Around this time the prince had also had an affair with Lady Hertford, and perhaps Maria used either (or both) of these as the excuse she needed to break off ties with the prince forever. They never spoke again but she continued to live quietly at Steine House on her annuity of £6,000 and other financial increases from the prince. On becoming King George IV he ordered that all evidence of this illegal marriage be destroyed, and when he died in 1830 he requested that the Duke of Wellington burn all the letters between Maria and himself. Maria asked that only four documents be saved. She met the duke and Lord Albermarle at her residence and handed over bundles of papers, and when she left, the duke remarked that she was the most honest woman he'd ever met. The two peers set about burning the letters, and it is claimed that five years later Wellington was still burning them, and the smell of burning paper and sealing wax filled the air. The fire also stained the white marble mantelpiece. The four documents saved were the mortgage on the Royal Pavilion, which the prince gave her, but of which she never took possession; her marriage certificate; a will the prince penned in 1796, a year after his marriage to Caroline of Brunswick, in which he said that Maria Fitzherbert was his true wife; and an affidavit from the clergyman who performed

St John's Catholic church in Kemptown where Maria Fitzherbert is buried (Conrad Hughes)

the wedding ceremony. These were deposited at Coutts Bank, and later deposited in the Royal Archives. Interestingly when George IV died he was wearing a locket around his neck containing a round miniature of Maria. She lived for seven years after him, and is buried in St John's Catholic church in Kemptown, the oldest Roman Catholic church in the area, which Maria had contributed to building. A monument showing Maria as a widow with the Lamp of Memory and kneeling before the broken gospels can be seen inside the church. Curiously she is wearing three wedding rings. Could this be her silent reminder to the world that she had three husbands?

❖ KINGLY VALE ❖

∞ *A sombre resting place* ∞

When the Danes sailed into Sussex, and landed near Chichester, the local Saxons were well prepared for the invasion. The Danes marched in force and were wiped out as recorded in the Anglo-Saxon Chronicles of AD 894. The narrow coombe at Kingly Vale is filled with sombre yew trees, some exceedingly old, and on the crest

Atmospheric Kingly Vale (Wiki Commons)

of Bow Hill stand four large barrows called the King's Graves or Devil's Humps, said to contain the remains of the leaders of the Viking invasion. The yew trees were planted to mark the site of the battle, but another story tells us that the Danes lie where they fell, their bones mingled under the roots, and their ghosts haunt the woods. Most agree that the woods are indeed haunted, but not with Danes but the ghosts of druids, and somewhere amid all the yew trees is a sacrificial oak waiting to be discovered. Others believe that the trees come to life, move and change shape in the dead of night. But whatever story you wish to remember, it is certainly not a place to visit or linger on a dark and misty night.

⚜ KIRDFORD ⚜

∞ *A sad end to a day* ∞

After a hard day's work, five young men, George Newman aged 17, Charles Newman aged 13, Thomas Rapley aged 14, George Puttick aged 13 and William Boxall aged 19, employed at Sladeland as houseboys, retired to the bedroom. Although it was a Sunday, it had been just another working day for them, except that it was a severely cold, bleak winter's day and they had returned freezing cold. The bedroom they occupied had no chimney, so to warm up the room they used to take a bucket of hot ashes from beneath the brick bread oven up to their room for warmth. Perhaps William, being the eldest, carried it up, and once they were all warm they climbed into bed and soon fell asleep. They would have left the green wood ashes to cool knowing that there was plenty of ventilation from the broken window in their room, but what they didn't know was that their employer must have felt sorry for them, and had had the window repaired. The following morning when they didn't report for duty we can imagine one of the servants being sent up to call them and finding all five had suffocated during the night. The tragic story unfolded:

> *To the memory of George Newman, aged 17, Charles Newman, aged 13, Thomas Rapley, aged 14, George Puttick, aged 13 and William Boxall, aged 19 years who died at Sladeland on the 21st of January, 1838, from having placed green wood ashes in their bedroom. In the midst of life we are in death.*

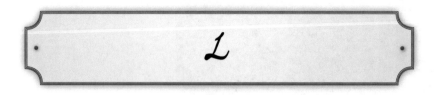

✦ LEWES ✦

∞ *Russian memorial to Finnish soldiers* ∞

You wouldn't expect to find a Russian memorial for Finnish soldiers in Sussex, but one stands as a reminder to the town that made them welcome. Not many people understood the reasoning behind the brutal Crimean War, least of all the soldiers forced to endure harsh Russian winters with little or no food. A long way from home, Finnish prisoners-of-war belonging to the Imperial Russian Army were in the Baltic fortress Bomarsund when it was captured by the British in 1854, and 340 of them were sent to England to await eventual repatriation. After all they had gone through they didn't quite know what to expect in yet another foreign country, but they had a pleasant surprise. On arrival the Russian officers were housed with local families and had the freedom to move around the town, whilst the soldiers, mostly Finnish conscripts, were confined within the prison walls, but were given facilities to make wooden toys to sell to visitors. Being handy with tools, they soon became a major attraction, with locals queuing to buy their wares. When the war ended, the prisoners returned to their original countries, but before leaving the commanding officer expressed his gratitude to the people of the town for their hospitality. Sadly twenty-eight didn't return home, having died at Lewes Naval Prison, which once stood near the site of the church. The obelisk erected in 1877 was given by Tsar Alexander II some twenty years afterwards, and bears the names of the prisoners and the inscription:

> Sacred to the memory of the Russian soldiers who died prisoners of war in Lewis in the years 1854, 1855 and 1856 and raised by order of His Majesty the Emperor of Russia Alexander II in 1877.

A popular Finnish folk-song, *Oolannin sota* (Crimean War), is said to have evolved from the earlier *Ålandin sota laulu* (War Song), which tells of their capture and

Russian memorial given by the
Tsar of Russia (Conrad Hughes)

imprisonment in Lewes, and is believed to have been written by one of the
prisoners during his internment. Their story was also the inspiration for *The
Finnish Prisoner*, set to the English language libretto written by Stephen Plaice,
who came across the story while he was writer-in-residence at the modern Lewes
Prison. It was composed by Orlando Gough and scored for a four-piece 'orchestra'
of violin, accordion, bass clarinet and vibraphone with three choruses, one for
children. When it was premiered in the town in 2007 to a sell-out audience,
Finland's ambassador to London attended. Both the church and the memorial are
designated Grade II listed buildings by English Heritage.

∾ *Did he really drive down Scare Hill?* ∾

George, Prince of Wales, was known to be wildly extravagant, but did his
exuberance run to driving a coach and four down Keere Street, also known as
Scare Hill, for a bet? We know he used to ride miles to see his beloved Maria
Fitzherbert, and as she lived in Clapham House at Litlington for awhile, just 7 miles
south east of Lewes, it could have occurred on one of his visits. The cobbled street
drops sharply downhill from the High Street towards Southover, and lies just

Plaque at Scare Hill – did the prince really drive down Scare Hill? (Richard Grieve)

outside the old town wall, forming the boundary for properties on the eastern side of the street. Most of the properties are Grade II listed, dating from the late eighteenth or nineteenth century and the street has gone down in history because of the famous legend that the Prince of Wales once drove down it.

⚜ LITLINGTON ⚜

∞ *An impulsive whim* ∞

One warm day in 1838 a group of farmers' sons decided they would take a boat trip to Alfriston, climb High and Over Hill and picnic on the top. James Pagden and his brothers from Frogfirle, and William Ade, a young cousin from Milton Court Farm, enjoyed their picnic and no doubt indulged in a few games, but soon became bored. One had an idea: why not cut a horse in the turf? After all, the coronation of Queen Victoria would take place in June, and how better to celebrate? 'Our horse will be there long after the celebrations,' they said, and so they set to work. Even little cousin William helped, and soon the horse was cut into the turf and remained on the chalky slope until the turn of the century. Some eighty-six years later John Ade was going for a walk on High and Over Hill with Mr Bovis, one of his farm workers, and Eric Hobbis, and starting talking about what they could do to make them famous before they died. All three had a good sense of humour and I expect much discussion took place, until John remembered his father helping to cut a horse in the turf, which had since disappeared, although the tales handed down in the family were still fresh. Although nothing now remained of the original horse John knew roughly where it had been, so why not cause a sensation with another, and better still, why not erect it overnight? At home John had a picture of the famous horse; he took a copy and drew a plan, and made careful measurements, because they wanted it to look good from a mile or more across the Cuckmere Valley. After much trial and error they felt they were ready to put their plan into action. They chose a cold and frosty night with a full moon, and armed with a bundle of wooden pegs and a new ball of twine they set off, arriving around seven in the evening. At first they hid in the bushes to make certain no-one was around, then set to work. With the aid of the pegs and the plan, they cut the soil as far as they could to make a clear outline. At 5 a.m. the task was complete, and they arrived home just in time to milk the cows. No doubt there were quite a few raised eyebrows that morning. During the Second World War the horse had to be camouflaged because of the possibility of enemy action, but only one of the horse's legs was put back, and by 1949 the horse needed to be renovated. Eric Hobbis had left the area, so John and his friend Bovis called on Harris, a builder's merchant, to help, and another night expedition took place on 9 June. It was further restored in 1983 when the forelegs were raised, giving the appearance of prancing instead of standing. Since 1991 it has been in the care of the National Trust who have scoured the outline several times. If John Ade wanted to be famous before he died, he certainly achieved his aim.

⁂ LOXWOOD ⁂

◌ *The Cocoa Drinkers* ◌

Today men and women living together is taken for granted, but when John Sirgood brought his unusual cult to West Sussex and formed co-operatives, it must have raised the odd eyebrow or two amongst the farming community and clergymen. It began in the 1840s when John settled in south London and became a disciple of William Bridges, founder of the Plumstead Peculiars. Shoemaker John preached widely around the area, but longed for a larger audience. One night in 1850, he dreamed that the Lord told him there were remote places in Sussex where men would listen to him. The next morning he closed his shop, and because he could not afford the train fare, bundled his possessions in a wheelbarrow, and lifting his wife Harriet on the top set off on the 41 mile walk to Loxwood. They took it in turns to push each other to their destination and must have received many a strange look as they progressed. He began his Christian sect with about five people and held meetings in one of the cottages. They called themselves the Society of Dependants. It was not easy at first, as they met opposition from the landed gentry and clergymen as they sought converts amongst the poorer classes. They were even threatened with action for holding unlawful meetings, but after many letters written by each side, the abolition of the Conventicle Act allowed them to worship openly. Within ten years more than half the local farmers and labourers had become members of his cult, and the first chapel was built at Loxwood using their combined savings. It was a simple undecorated building with a communal room behind. Members attended three services on Sunday and two during the week. They must have looked an eccentric bunch as they made their way across the fields and along the winding paths; the ladies wore black straw or velvet poke bonnets, black shawls, and black skirts that reached the ground, their hair always scraped back into a neatly plaited bun; the men were soberly dressed, with mutton chop whiskers and little beards under the chin, and Homburg felt hats. Between the morning and afternoon services those in the congregation who had come a long distance would assemble in a back room to rest. Tea was freely served, each person taking a meat pastry, cheese sandwich or whatever they fancied to sustain them though the day. Bank holiday days were spent travelling by hired motor coach or farm wagon to Loxwood for a special service. Interestingly, they became known as the Cokelers; when John preached in a village inn or nearby, the landlord would always ask if he would like some beer. 'No, but I will have some cocoa,' would come the reply, to the amusement of everyone, as at the time, it was little known in the country, and certainly not in rural Sussex., So the Cokelers, or the Cocoa Drinkers stuck. They stood out from other Christian sects as they did not use the Lord's Prayer, claiming that it was only given as a model for other prayers. They didn't listen to secular music, read secular books or play games, and didn't have wild flowers to adorn their humble homes. They never smoked or drank alcohol, but strangest of all was the fact that a strict Cokeler should not marry. They claimed a spouse stood between God and the Cokeler, who should be free of all earthly ties, but an arrangement was introduced whereby, having sought the approval of the elders, a trial marriage with the person of choice could take place. If after two years they both agreed then a lawful marriage would take place with the blessing of the chapel. With little or no opportunities for pleasure the Cokelers were obviously thrifty and hardworking, ploughing all their time and resources back into the community. In 1879 Loxwood opened its first Combination Store, where the Cokeler farmers not only sold their butter, milk and other produce to the store but also obtained all their necessities from the same place, thus keeping the money in the community. One of the hymns in their 'Dependants' Hymn Book' has the following verse:

Loxwood Combination Store, now a butchers shop (Conrad Hughes)

> Christ's Combination Stores for me
> Where I can be so well supplied,
> Where I can one with brethren be,
> Where competition is defied.

The store thrived and the members continued to invest in the enterprise, becoming shareholders and enjoying the benefits of good dividends. The staff lived above the shop, which meant as they were not in domestic service they were free to attend chapel on Sunday, It became a flourishing business with several departments, and by the 1920s Loxwood had a whole street of shops, a large garage and a steam bakery. John preached in private houses and outdoors all over England, and when his wife died nine years before him, he settled in another Cokeler village, Warnham, where he reverted to being a shoemaker. At the time of his death there were around 2,000 Cokelers in West Sussex, but today the name is barely known. It may have been a small insignificant cult outside Sussex, but no doubt their methods of selling within the community were copied in many a rural village.

First Cokeler's chapel, now Emmanuel Fellowship chapel (Conrad Hughes)

⚜ LYMINSTER ⚜

∞ *Who killed the Sussex Knucker?* ∞

Folklorists all agree that the Knucker was a nasty dragon that lived in a fathomless pool called Knucker Hole. It would fly through the air at speed and grab any flesh it could and take it back to be eaten alive. It ruled supreme until the King of Sussex said he would offer his daughter's hand in marriage to anyone who could slay the beast, and it is here that tales differ. Some say a gallant knight in shining armour stepped forward, tracked down the dragon, killed it, and married the princess and lived happily ever after. Others say that a farmer's lad, Jim Puttock, baked an enormous Sussex pie, and hauled it in a cart complete with horses into the Knucker Hole, then hid to see what happened. Unable to resist it, the Knucker soon gobbled the entire pie, cart, horses and all, and was promptly either overcome by a tummy ache, or keeled over and died. Unknown to the monster Jim had laced it with poison. Triumphant he rushed through the hedge and cut off the monster's head with a sickle. It had been thirsty work, so Jim went into the nearest ale house for a pint. Satisfied, he drew his hand across his mouth, but sadly some of the monster's blood was still on his hand, and it entered his body and he died. We may

St Mary Magdalene's church, home to the tomb of the dragon killer (Conrad Hughes)

never know who killed the Knucker, but the Slayer's Slab, reputed to be the tomb of the dragon killer, can be found in St Mary Magdalene's church. It is covered with a stone lid decorated with a cross and what could pass as dragon scales.

𝓜

✣ MARK CROSS ✣

෨ *Pioneering spirit* ෨

By the time Sophia Jex-Blake retired and bought Windydene, she had crammed more into her life than most people can even dream about, including becoming Scotland's first female doctor. She was born into a very wealthy religious family the year the Penny Black postage stamp was first issued, and lived at The Croft in Hastings. Maria, her mother, was not a well woman and found Sophia very difficult to handle. In a strict household things like dancing and theatregoing were forbidden, which her older brother and sister accepted; but Sophia was different. Full of energy and strong-willed, she often clashed with her parents, although she did have a loving relationship with them. At the age of 8 she attended a boarding school but became very frustrated when the school tried to teach her how to be a homemaker and eventual mother, things that were expected of Victorian ladies. She had a thirst for knowledge, little interest in marriage and preferred horse riding to more ladylike activities, and changed schools no fewer than six times in eight years. Unlike Sophia, her brother was given a good education, and in 1858 the rebellious young lady persuaded her father Thomas, a retired lawyer, to allow her at least a year's study at the Queen's College, London, one of the first colleges for women in England. She became interested in teaching and for the first time in her life she felt challenged; she enjoyed mathematics and went on to teach maths at the college, but her father didn't expect his daughter to earn a living and forbade her to take a salary. Sophia lived for a time with Octavia Hill's family and they formed a relationship and moved in together until Octavia broke it off, leaving Sophia devastated; but despite this they remained loyal friends. In 1861 Sophia finished at Queen's and returned home, and the following year enrolled at Edinburgh's Ladies' Educational Association in an attempt to get over the broken relationship. After travelling to Germany to teach at the Grand Ducal Institute for women in Mannheim, she became homesick and returned home for a year. In 1865 she talked her parents into allowing her to travel to the United States because she had heard of the co-education system and said, 'I have such a feeling that with the new world, a new life will open.' She was right. In Boston she met the pioneer physician, Lucy Sewell, and this was a turning point for Sophia. Despite having had no medical training she worked alongside Lucy and other doctors at the hospital, learning the practical work, especially diseases in women. Her experiences convinced her that she wanted to become a doctor and attend Harvard University, so in 1867 she and another trainee from the New England hospital wrote to the president and fellows of the university asking to be admitted to the medical school. They took a month to reply and it was not favourable. The letter stated, 'There is no provision for the education of women in any department of this university.' She then turned her hopes to joining the medical college being established by Elizabeth Blackwell in New York, but her father died and she returned home to be with her mother. She decided not to return to America but to pursue her medical training in the UK; Scotland had different attitudes, and she felt that if any university would allow women, then it would be a Scottish one. She applied in March 1869 to the medical faculty of the Senatus Academus, but again she was met with opposition, and although they voted in favour of allowing her to study medicine, the university court rejected her application on the grounds that the university could not make the necessary arrangements in the interests of just one lady. Sophia was made of stronger material, and immediately advertised in the *Scotsman* and national newspapers for more women to join her. A second application was submitted in the summer of that year on behalf of a group of five women initially, with two more joining later on in the year; they became known as the Edinburgh Seven. In her application Sophia requested the right to attend all the classes and examinations required for a degree in medicine, and this second application was approved by the university court, making the University of Edinburgh the first British university to admit women. The five women were admitted in 1870, but it was not easy for them. They had to attend separate classes and pay a higher fee than the men, but even so Sophia wrote to her good friend Lucy Sewell, 'It is a grand thing to enter the very first British university ever opened to women, isn't it?' When the men could see that the women could compete on equal terms with their male colleagues, so the hostility grew. The ladies were followed home, had mud thrown at them and fireworks attached to their front doors, and all this aggression developed into the Surgeon Hall Riot, when the women arrived for an anatomy exam and were greeted by an angry mob of over 200 men, blocking their entry and throwing mud and insults. The riot made national headlines, and won them numerous new supporters; however, members of the medical faculty put pressure on the university and they were refused graduation. Sophia led the women to file a lawsuit against the university for disallowing them the right to complete their medical training; they won, but lost on appeal. Again Sophia's strong personality shone through, and they finally took their cause to Parliament, where after a hard battle they succeeded, when a bill allowing all medical schools in Great Britain to admit women was passed, although some still wouldn't allow the women to take medical exams. Sophia completed her training at the University of Berne and was awarded her MD in January 1877. Four months later she qualified as Licentiate of the Kings and Queens College of Physicians in Ireland, meaning that at long last she could be registered with the General Medical Council, and became only the third woman doctor in the country to do so. The strong determination that had been such a problem to her parents and teachers had now helped her to win the right for women to receive a medical training. Jubilant, she returned to Edinburgh, proudly put up her brass plate in 1878, and Edinburgh had its first woman doctor. There was no stopping her now, and three months later she opened an outpatient clinic in Fountainbridge especially for women, who could receive medical treatment for a few pence. Her mother's death in 1881 had a devastating effect on Sophia, and she went through a period of depression, but despite this she still managed to set up the Edinburgh School of Medicine for Women and move her outpatient clinic to larger premises, adding a small five-bed ward. Scotland now had its first hospital for women, staffed entirely by women. Sophia finally retired at 59, and in 1889 she bought a house with 8 acres of land in Mark Cross, where she lived with a former pupil, Dr Margaret Todd, who became a novelist. Margaret had given up her medical career after only five years to be with Sophia, and despite

Sophia Jex-Blake at the age of 25

an age difference of some twenty years they lived happily together, tending a herd of cows and a kitchen garden, and looking after an orchard where they grew peaches, figs and grapes. Sophia had great sympathy with ladies; she supported the suffragettes, and organised a campaign against the speeding motor car, having noticed whilst out in her carriage that they filled the village with dust and noise. The two women spent their time reading, travelling and entertaining, and their home became a meeting place for former students and colleagues, as well as writers and acquaintances from all over the world. In her later years Sophia suffered a series of heart attacks and died in January 1921 at the age of 71. She willed all her possessions, including her personal papers and diaries, to Margaret, who wrote a biography, *The Life of Sophia Jex-Blake*, in 1918, and after the book was published in accordance with Sophia's wishes she destroyed all her personal papers including her voluminous diaries in which she chronicled her entire life. Just three months later Margaret committed suicide at the age of 58, and both she and Sophia are buried nearby at St Denys church, Rotherfield.

❖ MAYFIELD ❖

∞ *Learned or eccentric?* ∞

I expect like most people John (Pigtail) Bridger had two different sides to his character. His fame spread for miles, and depending on who was telling the tale, he was either a cynical wizard who delighted in casting spells on his victims, or a very learned, kind, well-respected farmer who had studied theology and history. John, born in 1794, was the son of a yeoman farmer, and acquired his nickname from the enormous pigtail he wore almost down to the waist, tied with a white silk ribbon. His side whiskers were also plaited. He married his first cousin Mary Bridger in 1827 and fathered five children, Augustus Caesar, Cicero Caius, Virgil Edward, Octavia Echo, and Venus Pandora. Local folklore tells us that when he brought his son to be baptised, the clergyman was startled when he requested that the child be named Beelzebub. The vicar refused to saddle a child with the name. 'But, sir, the name is in the Bible, and you are therefore bound to use it.' The clergyman advised that the baptismal party should adjourn to the graveyard to think things over while he conducted the ordinary afternoon service, and then returned to the church where the baptismal service took place. Sometime later Bridger returned and the child was baptised with the name Augustus Caesar. John loved dressing up as a tramp on his own land and would allow himself to be arrested for vagrancy. A policeman new to the village saw a ragged man crouching over a fire on Bridger's land and was about to take him before the magistrate for trespassing when Bridger stood up, towering over the policeman and roared, 'I'll trouble you not to come interfering with my land in future.' On another occasion he carried a cannonball he'd found on the beach at Eastbourne back to Mayfield just to see what it would look like in his garden, a distance of some 25 miles. He was said to have had bars fitted to all his windows in order to keep the Devil out, and these tales were always considered folklore until, in the 1950s, a 50lb cannonball was unearthed in his old garden; furthermore after building renovation started on his house, they peeled away the old plaster from the window sills and found that originally bars had been fitted across and then sawn off. He also walked all the way to London to see the Crystal Palace Exhibition of 1851 with his wife and children. Once there, he left them to wander among the costumes and other objects while he went in search of the machinery. Engrossed in the exhibition, he forgot all about his family. Eventually a policeman tapped him on the shoulder and told him his family were asking for him. 'And pray, how come you found me among these thousands of people?' enquired Bridger. The policeman hesitated for a few seconds. 'Well, you see, sir, you are not dressed just like other people.' I don't suppose it was the long white smock that the well-to-do farmers wore with knee breeches and gaiters on Sunday, but his sheer height and his fiery red hair tied halfway down his back made him distinctive. Pigtail was known to have a terrifying hypnotic stare which could apparently freeze a man to the spot, and it is claimed that he could cast a spell on anyone and would only release it when he had had his fun. On his small farm he employed four labourers, and loved to punish them in this way whenever they argued with him or were slacking in their work, or any other way that displeased him. He would usually wait until meal times, and as the labourers came through the door famished after a hard day he called them in, but just as they stepped over the threshold, as swift as lightning he would cast his spell, leaving the men riveted to the spot in sight of the food and the delicious smells hitting their nostrils. Pigtail would then proceed to taunt the poor labourers by smiling, waving his forkful of food before eating it slowly. When he tired of his game he would release the spell and invite them in to eat. One final oddity: in 1848 Pigtail built a fine house at Mayfield but refused to live in it or let anyone else buy it. It stayed empty until his death in 1876.

⚜ MIDHURST ⚜

෨ *The Etonian who became a gentleman of the road* ෨

Born into a wealthy and well-connected family in 1662, Robert Congden was a Sussex man who enjoyed being bad. His father had great plans for young Robert. First came a good education; he went off to Eton 1675, then on to King's College in Cambridge. We are not sure what happened to change Robert, but he never stood out at school and wasted his time at university on self-indulgence, buying gaudy clothes and fine wines, and more often seen in inns than in the lecture halls or libraries, like many young men from privileged backgrounds. In those days it was possible to obtain a degree simply by staying at college for a minimum of three years. His father give him a generous allowance of £80 a quarter whilst he stayed at university, but he was a spendthrift, and only kept company with undergraduates who were strapped for cash or the ruffians of the city, but as he was always well dressed, he attracted many an honest, upright young lady as well as the immoral kind. Naturally he was soon in debt and being chased by creditors, and when his allowance from his father failed to arrive, Robert hit upon the idea of 'taking a purse or two', as he put it, and due to the close proximity of the Sport of Kings at Newmarket, there were plenty of rich victims for him. Having made the decision to make easy money he put his plan into action, and bought himself a couple of dangerous-looking cocked pistols. Then one cold, wet November afternoon, near to the racecourse's famous Rowley Mile, he took up his position, but the ambush went terribly wrong. Along came a mounted traveller, Caleb Pilbeam, and Robert spurred his horse, raised his pistols and uttered the words, 'Stand and deliver!' Caleb was not going to hand over his money, and drew his sword, urging his horse towards Robert. In panic Robert fired his pistols; one misfired but the other sent the ball straight into Caleb's heart. Robert robbed the man of a considerable amount of cash and valuables and coolly rode back to Cambridge and his college lodgings. When he arrived he opened the bag to find a letter, and discovered that he had killed his father's courier, who had come to deliver his belated quarterly allowance. This played on his mind, and he was worried that he would somehow be linked to the crime. He decided he would leave the country, and packed his belongings and fled to Holland. We will never know how he explained this to his father, who continued to pay him an allowance of £100 a year, more than enough for him to carry on indulging his vices in Amsterdam. Maybe he supplemented his allowance with further crime. It's unclear, but we do know that in 1685 he was recruited by Charles II's illegitimate son the Duke of Monmouth as a soldier in his rebel army which arrived in England with a corrupt army full of criminals and doubtful characters like Robert. However, his devotion did not last long and he deserted before the Battle of Sedgmoor. Instead he slipped quietly back to Midhurst to see his father, but too late; his father had just died, and he found himself a very rich man. However, under a condition of his father's will he would only inherit if he carried on running the family Sussex farms and estate. He tried his hand at going straight, but he didn't like hard work; the life of a farmer was not for him. Soon he took up his old ways and frequented the taverns in Midhurst and Chichester, living a double existence for two years as a respectable farmer by day and thief by night. Mounted on a thoroughbred and wearing a long black cloak with solid silver fastenings, carrying a silver hilted sword and a pair of the finest Dutch pistols money could buy, he looked the part of a highwayman. His career spanned only four years, but in that time he robbed scores of travellers and rich

The historic market town of Midhurst (Conrad Hughes)

merchants in ever widening circles, taking in East Sussex and Surrey as well as the outskirts of London. He took pleasure in robbing a lawyer on his way back from Lewes Assizes, and many thought he was a foreigner because he spoke perfect Dutch. His fame spread as the mysterious eloquent dresser with the funny accent, but he was no Dick Turpin; he was ruthless, and would slit the traveller's horse's throat, leaving him to walk miles to seek help or shelter. One day, his luck ran out when he robbed the Earl of Dorset, getting away with 1,000 guineas, but this time Robert could not slip back into being the country gentleman. The earl demanded the blood of his assailant, and fuelled by a handsome reward, a sharp thief-taker looking for a quick buck saw him in a tavern drinking and gambling heavily. After a struggle he dragged Robert to the notorious Newgate Prison; although he confessed to his deeds the authorities were reluctant to commit gentry to trial, but he was sent before the judge and was hanged in 1691 at the age of 29 for the first of his crimes, that of killing Caleb Pilbeam at Newmarket Heath.

⚜ NEWHAVEN ⚜

◎ HMS Brazen – a sad disaster ◎

With its dramatic coastline, Newhaven is no stranger to disasters, but one of the saddest in the town's maritime history must be the loss of HMS *Brazen*, on 26 January 1800, which claimed 105 lives and left only one survivor. Commander James Hanson RN was an experienced young officer who had sailed with Edward Vancouver to the Americas, and it seems so tragic that his brilliant career should have been cut short so abruptly on these treacherous rocks. On 16 January HMS *Brazen* left Portsmouth with a crew of 120 to sail between the naval base at St Helen's on the Isle of Wight and Beachy Head 'to protect trade and annoy the enemy'. Only the previous day off the Isle of Wight she had met a small French ship, which had turned on its heels, but the *Brazen* used all possible sails and soon caught up and took it without a struggle. Captain Hanson was particularly pleased with himself, because the capture had been swift, and he placed on board his first mate, a midshipman, eight ordinary seaman and two marines, who then sailed her to Portsmouth, no doubt looking forward to a share of the prize money. This action ultimately saved the lives of those sailors aboard the prize, but may have left the *Brazen* under-manned to deal with the gale ahead. The story begins to unfold on the evening of 25 January when HMS *Brazen* was sailing eastwards into wind followed by heavy squally rain. The ship managed to clear Selsey Bill. Early the following morning at 6 a.m. word was received that a large ship was on the shore under the cliffs at Newhaven. An express message was sent to Captain Andrew Sproule RN at Brighton, who was in command of this part of the coastal defences, and local fishermen, sailors, dock workers and others rushed to the shore, where they could hear the mariners' pitiful screams. The flood tide came in so fast that there was little they could do to help them. Two lifting cranes were brought to the top of the cliff with the aid of eight oxen, ready to save lives once the tide had receded. By now the *Brazen*'s masts had fallen overboard, and all the spectators could see were desperate mariners clinging on to parts protruding from the sea. Two men jumped into the lifting cage and were lowered down the 300ft cliff to rescue those floating on the waves. One man drifted towards them, but as they came to his assistance, part of a loose sail threw him overboard and he disappeared. They noticed another man lashed to a gun-slide being washed ashore; they grabbed him, and he turned out to be the only survivor. Sadly no further rescue attempts could be made because it would have endangered the lives of the rescuers. Wagons came from Newhaven and took the bodies away, and a few days later the wreck broke up and disappeared forever. By February, the sole survivor, Jeremiah Hill, was fit enough to tell his tale. He recalled that he came on watch at 10 p.m. on the Sunday night, and during his watch the wind blew up to a full-scale gale from the south west and showed no sign of abating. He was relieved at 2 a.m., but due to the conditions he didn't go down to his hammock until 4 a.m., and lay there so exhausted that he didn't even have the energy to remove his boots. At 5 a.m. a terrific crash roused him from half-sleep as the ship struck the rocks. He raced up on deck with his jacket and trousers still in his hand to find the ship sinking, the waves breaking over the deck. He had no time to put either garment on and became part of a team under John Teague, the ship's carpenter, cutting through the weather shrouds to let the main and mizzen masts go. Captain Hanson gave the order to abandon ship, and he and the purser, Mr Braugh, threw themselves into the water and were never seen again. Together with thirteen mariners Jeremiah Hill, unable to swim, lagged behind unsure what to do next, then suddenly the mast crashed on to the decks and the ship was pushed on to her side. There wasn't even time to fire a distress signal. Jeremiah found the stump of the foremast and clung on desperately as the sky lightened a little and the dark shape of the shore came into view. After a while he noticed a large gun-slide or carriage tethered to a mounting post; he threw himself on to the slide and cut it free to allow it to drift into the sea. As late as May of that year, bodies continued to be washed up. Ninety-five bodies were washed ashore in all, and the Admiralty provided rough coffins that were interred at St Michael's churchyard at Newhaven. Ten bodies, including that of Captain Hanson and the purser, were never recovered; Hanson's wife offered a reward for the recovery of the captain's body, which could be identified by the tattoo of an anchor picked out in gunpowder on his arm. We know the ship was lost in January 1800, but there appears to be some confusion with the exact date; 20 January is etched on the monument, but according to the *Sussex Advertiser* dated 27 January, the event took place 'yesterday morning', making it 26 January. It could be that the monument was erected some months after the disaster and a genuine mistake was made due to difficulty with the handwriting, resulting in 26 being confused for 20. The monument towers over the town of Newhaven and is a fitting reminder of Newhaven's biggest shipping disaster. At the time Captain Hanson's wife was pregnant, and on 5 May 1800 a son, James Hawsey Hanson, was born to Louisa at Dartford. Sadly on 17 May 1802 the little boy died, just twelve days after his second birthday. When James was drowned Louisa was just 20 years old. She never remarried, but lived to the grand age of 103 and drew a Naval Officers' Widows' Pension for eighty three years, the longest-recorded pension in naval history. The Sussex song, *The Wreck of the* Brazen, was composed by an inhabitant of Bishopstone in the year 1800, and sung in the Newhaven port area, becoming very popular amongst mariners and fishermen. A copy of the song, given to him by his father, belonged to Mr Walter Eager, one of the watch house staff. It was published in 1911, possibly by the *East Sussex News*, although to date it has been impossible to confirm this.

THE WRECK OF THE *BRAZEN*

You seaman all, pray give attention
To these few lines which I am going to tell:
A shocking story I will tell you,
That on the *Brazen* sloop it fell.

It happened on one Sunday morning,
On January th' twenty-six,
On the high rocks near to Newhaven
The *Brazen* sloop-of-war did fix.

And when she struck 'twas at low water,
About the turning of the tide;
To tell the power of wind and water
No man was able to describe.

How shocking 'twas to hear the screaming,
The crew so loud for help did cry;
Her masts and rigging were torn to pieces,
Like chaff before the wind did fly.

How shocking 'twas to behold them
That morning when they came on shore:
Pieces of timber, likewise dead bodies
From the *Brazen* sloop the water bore.

Soon their boats were broke to pieces,
Their precious lives they tried to save;
'Twas all in vain, it proved so fatal,
They sank into a watery grave.

The only survivor of the *Brazen*, Jeremiah Hill, being winched to safety (Royal Humane Society, by kind permission of Seaford Museum and Heritage Society)

Out of a hundred and sixteen seamen
Only one poor soul got safe to shore;
So shocking was the wreck of the *Brazen*,
The like was never seen before.

Captain Hanson and his lieutenant
Both stripped and tried to swim ashore,
But sad to say they were exhausted –
Drowned they were and could swim no more.

Captain Hanson has left a widow,
All in distress for to weep;
Like many more on board with him
They all were perished in the deep.

Some had watches, some had money,
Gold rings around their fingers, too;
Some had wives and some had sweethearts –
In sorrow did lament it's true.

Memorial in St Michael's church to HMS *Brazen* (Conrad Hughes)

Now to conclude and finish my ditty;
A mournful tale throughout my song
May God protect all British seamen
That on the raging seas belong.

How shocking 'twas to behold them –
The force of gale it did increase;
There were many on the cliff stood gazing,
But they could render no relief.

May the bright angels rule the ocean
And safely seamen for to guide!
Not like the *Brazen* that was condemned
Upon Newhaven rocks to ride.

Every year on the anniversary of the sinking of HMS *Brazen* a memorial service is held at St Michael's church, standards paraded, and wreaths laid in honour of the crew. A lone bugler sounds the Last Post and Reveille.

∞ *The town's infamous guest* ∞

Charles Deville Wells will go down in history as the man who broke the bank at Monte Carlo. In July 1891 the tubby gambling cockney went to the casino at Monte Carlo, the only place in Europe where gambling was permitted. He arrived at midday and went straight to the roulette table, and eleven hours later had broken the bank. In the course of a week he broke the bank no fewer than twelve times and won £40,000, worth around £4 million today. Professional detectives were hired to discover his system, but to make matters worse on another trip later that year he made a further killing. Charles claimed his wins were down to sheer bravery and guts, and said anyone was free to watch him play. Legend informs us that Charles and his French mistress were regular guests at the London and Paris Hotel in the town, and would regularly stop there when they travelled between Britain and France. They were always holding parties which went on into the early hours of the morning and kept all the other visitors awake. Finally the pair were asked to take their business elsewhere and rented a house in nearby Fort Road where the parties continued.

❖ NINFIELD ❖

∞ *Made from local iron* ∞

Most village stocks were made of wood with an iron lock, but those at Ninfield are unusual because they are made of iron and also have a whipping post attached. They were most probably made at the Ashburnham Forge in the next village. There are four holes in the stocks for the ankles and on the upright post are four wrist clamps, just to make sure that the felon did not escape. He would have

Unusual iron stocks at Ninfield (Conrad Hughes)

spent a most uncomfortable day in the stocks being pelted with rotting fruit and vegetables. This was also a time when divorce was not an option for poorer people but there was the tradition of wife-selling. She would have been dragged to the stocks with a halter around her neck and sold to the highest bidder. The last such deal struck at Ninfield was in 1790 when a wife was sold for a pint of gin, but it is also claimed that the next day, presumably when the husband had sobered up and realised her usefulness was worth more than he was paid, he had a change of heart and bought her back for more than he had received.

⚘ NORTHIAM ⚘

∽ *A long way from home* ∽

Mystery surrounds a perfectly preserved ancient vessel, discovered in 1822 in a field near the River Rother at Northiam. At the time it was assumed that it belonged to Danish invaders, and probably sank in the ninth century. History informs us that in the year AD 892, 250 Viking ships came up the river, destroying a fort under construction before the Vikings moved on. They then set up camp at Appledore in Kent, until King Alfred and his army removed them. The waterway would have been much wider then, but over time it was changed to land or shrunk to the dimensions of the present stream. The Sussex historian Thomas Horsfield, who wrote *The History Antiquities and Topography of the County of Sussex*, examined the vessel, and said, 'Her dimensions were, from head to stern, 65 feet, and her width 14 feet, with cabin and forecastle; and she appears to have originally had a whole deck. In her caulking was a species of moss peculiar to the country in which she was built.' In the cabin and other parts of the vessel were found a human skull with a pair of goat's horns attached to a part of the cranium; a dirk or poniard, about half an inch of the blade of which had resisted corrosion; several parts of sandals, two earthenware jars and a stone mug. Horsfield also added, 'There was a piece of board exhibiting about thirty perforations, probably designed for keeping lunar months, or for some game or amusement.' Unfortunately neither the ship nor the artefacts listed by Horsfield have survived, but a print, discovered at the Science Museum, shows the vessel as she lay at the time of excavation and offers a different perspective on the find. With better knowledge and with the print showing a well-preserved rudder still hanging from the stern-post, it is now thought the vessel was no earlier than thirteenth century. As the Rother lies a little below Bodiam Castle, which was built in 1386, and we know that the stone was brought up the river by ship, if it had survived it might well have been the only example of a medieval coaster. What is more intriguing is why an eminent historian like Horsfield should be so precise about the species of moss in the ship's caulking, which he stated came from Denmark.

⊹ NUTLEY ⊹

∾ *In sight of Bow Bells* ∾

During the eighteenth century all roads led to London, and along the A22 and A26 numerous mileposts can be spotted including one at Nutley. The longest line of milestones can be found on the A22, which stretches from Lingfield in Surrey to Hailsham. They are all made of iron and have a string of bells under a single bow, and a figure to signify the number of miles from Bow Bells church in London. The relief of a buckle at the top of the number represents the Pelham family. In 1356 at the Battle of Poitiers, local knight Sir John Pelham together with Sir Roger de la Warr were instrumental in the capture of John II, King of France, and Sir John was given the king's buckle as a badge of honour by the Black Prince, Edward III.

Milepost at Nutley
(Wiki Commons)

⚜ OVINGDEAN ⚜

∽ *Trail blazer with many firsts* ∽

Helena Normanton will always be remembered as the first woman to practise as a barrister, the first to obtain a divorce for a client, the first to lead the prosecution in a murder trial, the first to conduct a trial in America and the first to represent cases at the High Court and Old Bailey. She was also one of the first two women to become a King's Council, the highest appointment given to a barrister, and yet today, sixty years after she died, very few know her name and there is no statue to celebrate her many achievements. She was born in 1882, and perhaps it was her early struggles that gave her the motivation to stand out in a man's world. At the age of 4, her piano tuner father was found dead with a broken neck in a railway tunnel, and she moved from London to Brighton with her mother and younger sister. To make ends meet her mother ran a grocery shop, and turned the family home in Clifton Place into a boarding house, and things looked promising for the young Helena when at the age of 14 she won a scholarship to York Place Science School, a forerunner of Varndean School for Girls. But just four years later her mother died and she had to leave school to look after her sister and help run the business. In 1901 they moved to Hove, to live at a boarding house in Hampton Place, and two years later she was able to resume her studies. For some reason she went to the Edge Hill Teachers' Training College in Liverpool, possibly because it had gained a reputation as a college of strong female culture, had connections with the suffragette movement, and was a well respected college. After qualifying in 1905 she taught history in Glasgow and London, and was rarely without work, but she had always held the ambition to one day become a barrister. In 1918 she applied to become a student at Middle Temple; initially she was refused, but the determined Helena lodged a petition with the House of Lords, and was admitted in 1919 after her reapplication within hours of the Sex Disqualification (Removal) Act. As expected from a woman who was making her way into male-dominated territory, she also became a strong supporter of women's rights, and joined the Women's Social and Political Union (WSPU), but soon became one of the seventy women who, disenchanted with the leadership of Emmeline and

Christabel Pankhurst, broke away and formed the Women's Freedom League. She also supported the campaign of the Women's Peace Council for a negotiated peace during the First World War, and became an early member of CND. Equality of pay was also an issue close to her heart, and despite having a successful legal career, she had to supplement her income by letting out rooms in her house and writing for newspapers and magazines to make ends meet. As early as 1914 she asked the question in a pamphlet titled *Sex Differentiation in Salary*, 'Should women be paid according to their sex or their work?' I wonder what she'd think today, to know that what she described in such black and white terms should still be something that many women are denied. She married Gavin Bowman Watson Clark in 1921, and in 1924 attracted a great deal of attention as well as much disapproval, when

Helena's grave
in St Wulfran's
churchyard,
Ovingdean
(Conrad Hughes)

she won the right to keep her maiden name in practice, unheard of in those days, and became the first married woman to be granted a passport in her maiden name. She was also a strong campaigner for women's rights within marriage, believing that once married, men and women should be equal, and in the 1930s campaigned for changes in the matrimonial law to allow married men and women to keep their money and property separately. She must have outraged her generation by daring to suggest that if women saved money out of their housekeeping, then it was theirs, and they were entitled to spend it as they wished, even, suggesting the unthinkable, on cigarettes. In 1938, despite hostility from the Mothers' Union, with Vera Brittain, Edith Summerskill and Helen Nutting she co-founded the Married Women's Association, and was their president until 1952. She always maintained her links with Brighton throughout her life, and was the first person to donate funds for the establishment of Sussex University. In 1999 a portfolio of shares worth in excess of £400,000 was passed to the university on the death of one of her relations. Her ashes are buried near those of her husband, in the churchyard at Ovingdean, and it seems so unjust that for someone who did so much for women in life that her memorial does not justify her achievements.

❧ PAGHAM ❧

∽ *Code name Mulberry* ∽

The story of the D-Day invasion and the Mulberry Harbours built in northern France are familiar to everyone, but what may be not so well known is the role Pagham played in its success. After the disaster of the Dieppe Raid in 1942, all major ports were fiercely defended by the German forces, which created a problem: how could troops and their necessary supplies be transported across the Channel? It was decided to build two artificial harbours, Mulberry A for the Americans at St Laurent, and Mulberry B at Arromanches for the British, and because nothing this large had been attempted before, many people had to research and build these structures, and in the end over 300 experiments took place. The tides and depth of the water were essential to the operation, and tests were carried out to make sure that these man-made harbours would be able to hold up in bad weather and varying circumstances. The harbours would be used to bring food, ammunition and fuel to the troops, and it was estimated that the amount of equipment required by each soldier would be around 20lbs, amounting to 600 tons of supplies needed per day. Finally they agreed that floating caissons or bottomless concrete watertight chambers, made in sections, would be constructed by civil engineer contractors working around the coast of Britain, and sunk prior to D-Day, then refloated or 'resurrected' (hence the name phoenixes), and towed across the Channel in pieces to be assembled on site. Hundreds were stored in the sea off Pagham harbour and as there were no moorings available they were flooded and sunk temporarily to be pumped out and raised when needed. But though this was a sound idea in principle, there wasn't enough manpower, the pumps were not up to the task and the pumps didn't fit into the holes. With D-Day fast approaching, the task was passed to the salvage department of the navy who sent men, air compressors and pumps from all over country to help. In the end enough were raised to keep up with the demand. It must have been a unique sight for those watching to see 140 tugs leave Aldwick Bay, towing rafts carrying various Mulberry structures, but things didn't go smoothly, and at least one of these phoenixes sank. Later the ballast tank

Overlord Memorial at Pagham harbour (Conrad Hughes)

Salt House at Pagham, now a tourist information centre (Conrad Hughes)

was pumped out to re-float it for the invasion, but thanks to a SNAFU (military term for Situation Normal, All F★★★★d Up), the tugs were not ready and it had to be re-sunk. In the process it swung, and broke its back, and settled on the seabed. In 1999 a memorial to commemorate the men who made this possible and Pagham's role in the D-Day landings was erected on the beach in direct line with the phoenix that sank offshore and is visible at low tide. In all fifty had been assembled between Pagham beach and Selsey.

෨ *Salt me down* ෨

At the head of the harbour sits a small thatched-roof building, known as the Salt House, a remnant from the past, now used as an information centre. Without fridges and freezers, salt was essential to preserve food for times when it was not readily available. During the 1800s most families maintained a small garden for growing vegetables, and would also keep a pig. When the time came to slaughter the animal, the lean parts were shared with neighbours on the understanding they would return the favour when their own pig was slaughtered. This left the fatty parts, and each cottage would have a pork tub and salt down these parts to see them though the cold winter months.

⚜ PEACEHAVEN ⚜

∽ *Where east meets west* ∽

Peacehaven didn't exist until late 1915, when British-born but Canadian-raised businessman Charles Neville created the town by buying up barren land and a row of coastguard cottages. With its ideal setting near the sea, the town became the home for retiring veterans of the First World War. It also meant that because the land was cheap, working-class families from London could purchase plots and build weekend or holiday homes. Neville was a man with few principles, always on the lookout for ways to generate publicity, and he ran national competitions with plots of land as prizes. One such competition was to choose a name for the town, with a first prize of £100 and fifty second prizes of £50 building plots. There were over 80,000 suggestions, and the name New Anaz on Sea was chosen, as the Australia and New Zealand Army Corp ran a training camp in the area. However, after the defeat at Gallipoli in 1916, the name was quietly changed to Peacehaven in 1917. In 1933 local resident Commander Davenport RN realised that the town lay on the Greenwich Meridian. Neville saw an opportunity and asked Davenport to organise a public appeal to raise money for a monument complete with a drinking fountain, which would mark both the Meridian and commemorate the forthcoming Silver Jubilee of King George V in June 1936. A forerunner to the monument, a concrete strip some fifty yards long, was to run from the promenade to the cliff edge showing distances to several well-known capital cities. The appeal was officially launched on 10 August 1935, and a correspondent from *The Times* newspaper turned the first sod and unveiled a model of the proposed memorial. The date coincided with the 260th anniversary of the laying of the first foundation stone of the Royal Observatory at Greenwich, and was reported in the *Times* two days later, but unfortunately the king died on 20 January, before the foundation stone had been laid. The ever resourceful Neville quickly decided to rename it the King George V Memorial and Prime Meridian Obelisk. Neville laid the foundation stone on 30 May. The appeal was to raise £3,000, and the souvenir programme containing a list of eighty-four names and one anonymous donation raised £111 14s. The monument was unveiled on Saturday 8 August 1936, with the newly appointed Astronomer Royal Harold Spencer Jones delivering a speech. During the 1960s the monument was again moved 30ft north from its original position when work on the coastal defence was carried out because of cliff erosion. The first phase in the construction of a new sea wall and groynes began in 1977, and in August 1981 the local paper *Meridian Post* reported that the monument was to be moved back another 24ft from the cliff edge, because the cliff was to be trimmed back as part of a new phase of the works. The second move was

Meridian Monument overlooking the cliffs at Peacehaven (Conrad Hughes)

less straightforward than the first because the land on which the obelisk stood belonged to the town, whereas the new site belonged to Lewes District Council. Suggestions that the obelisk should be moved nearer the Meridian Centre were apparently considered but rejected, because the town's logo shows it on the cliff top and because it was also regarded as a maritime navigation aid. The monument became the focal point of the town's celebrations when the centenary of the Meridian was celebrated in 1984, but it was damaged in the storms of 1987 when the globe on its top was lost to the sea; it has since been replaced.

⁂ PEASE POTTAGE ⁂

∞ *Has it always been a resting place?* ∞

Pease Pottage is well known for its motorway service station and stopping point, and that may have always been the case. Tradition informs us that convicts on their way from London to the south coast, perhaps to be transported to Tasmania, or moved from East Grinstead to Horsham Gaol, were allowed to stop here to rest, and were given a bowl of pottage, a mash of boiled peas eaten with a slice of pork – hence the unusual name.

⚜ PEVENSEY ⚜

∾ *Consumed by jealousy* ∾

They say jealousy is the root of evil and this is certainly true of rich merchant Thomas Dight. He had taken a mistress, Eleanor Fitzjohn, who was many years his junior, and he needed to find a place for her to stay when he was away. He heard that the old Mint House, now no longer producing coins, was available to rent as the owner was abroad, and he felt it was the perfect love nest for him and Eleanor. Being a merchant, Thomas was away a great deal on business, and the young woman would spend many days alone waiting for him to return. And being young and energetic, Eleanor felt she was wasting her life, until she met a young local fisherman. He was not only handsome but unattached too, and so an affair began. But fate was not on the side of the young couple. One evening Thomas returned unexpectedly and found his mistress in bed with a stranger. His jealousy knew no bounds, and he ranted in the bedchamber. Then he sat down, decided on their punishment and proceeded to carry it out, enlisting a number of his henchman. He was rich and they were loyal so they carried out his punishment to the letter. All night long they were ordered to throw light from burning flame torches on to the walls creating eerie distorted images, as the couple cowered naked beneath the blankets. Eleanor desperately tried to calm him, no doubt familiar with his anger, and even left her lover's side to whisper endearments into Thomas's ears, but to no avail. He lashed out with the back of his hand, sending her flying across the room. She scrambled to her feet and tried again, but this time Thomas sent her flying into a corner. Then he ordered his servants to bind her securely as the horrified fisherman was restrained and forced to watch as poor Eleanor's tongue was cut out, before she was carried into what was once the minting chamber with their walls of solid stone and the chimney that took the strong fumes from the molten metal out into the open. Various items used in the manufacturing of coins were still in the room. Thomas noticed chains fixed to the ceiling, so he calmly had the fisherman dragged into the room and gagged, so he could not cry out, and tied each of his limbs to the chains. Face down, naked and spread-eagled, like a bird in flight, the fisherman hung in mid-air and swung from side to side. There was plenty of wood in the house, so a fire was built underneath the fisherman on the stone floor, and Thomas applied the torch to the kindling. When the fire began to take hold Thomas calmly sat down and watched Eleanor's lover roast alive. Once the flames caught it should have been a quick ending, but the wood was damp, and the fire was slow and smoky. In fact it became so smoky that Thomas and his companions had to leave the room. It may have been the smoke that finally killed the fisherman. When he was dead they cut him down in the middle of the night and threw him over the parapet of the village bridge for the tide to take him out to sea. We can assume that because fishing was a dangerous occupation, no questions were asked, as fishermen often went missing and never returned. Eleanor was carried to an upper room where she was left to die, still tied up, and obviously having lost a great deal of blood was in no state to try to escape. She was left with no food or water and the doors locked. We can only hope she died quickly. Thomas returned to the house after a while and removed her body and buried it behind the Mint House. No-one enquired about Eleanor, and everyone assumed that she'd simply moved on to a new lover. There the story would have ended, but in 1603 Thomas Dight was on his deathbed and wishing to make peace with his Maker, confessed his evil deeds to friends and a priest.

The old Mint House at Pevensey

PIDDINGHOE

✂ *Little Edith's Treat* ✂

The small village of Piddinghoe, like many others in Sussex, has in its church a benefactor's board recording its local charities. Here, however, is a rather sad tale about the founding of a charitable event – Little Edith's Treat. The origins of the custom derive from a distraught grandmother called Elizabeth Croft, who after her husband died in 1866 took solace in the birth of her granddaughter. But on 19 July 1868, little Edith died when she was only thirteen weeks old. In honour of her memory Elizabeth established a fund. On 19 July each year, a small payment was made from the fund, and the treat followed the same pattern each year. In the afternoon of what would have been her birthday, the schoolchildren were told the story of the bequest, before attending a church service. Then they were taken to an open space called the Hoe where various games and races took place, finishing with tea which, in the days when food may have been scarce, was a real treat. Sometime during the afternoon the vicar would also throw a handful of coins into the air for the children to scramble for, and prizes and gifts were distributed back at the school. There were awards to the boys for tidiness, and for those who attended school and church regularly. The girls competed for prizes for needlecraft, and by 1904 seventy local schoolchildren enjoyed a grand tea party with biscuits, sweets and nuts. But sadly the school closed in 1952, and although the custom moved naturally to Sunday school, a fall in child numbers and decrease in the annual value of the fund meant the 'treat' became irregular. In the 1990s it ceased as a formal event, but money was still available for one-offs. For example, in 2000 some of the money paid for a Christmas party, so despite the loss of the actual day the gift still continues when there is enough money available. I am sure that Elizabeth Croft would approve.

✥ PLAYDEN ✥

✂ *Unusual memorial* ✂

The old twelfth-century church of St Michael and All Angels in the little hamlet of Playden is home to a rather unusual memorial, that of a sixteenth-century Flemish brewer. Cornelis Roetmans, fleeing from Spanish persecution in the Low Countries, settled in the area along with a community of Huguenots, and continued his business as a brewer. When he died in 1530 he was suitably remembered by a memorial slab of black stone carved with beer barrels and a crossed matchstick fork, the tools he would have used in life, which were originally inlaid with brass.

PLUMMERS PLAIN

∽ *Money Mound* ∽

This unusual mound in a farm field gained its name after the rabbits who had inhabited it for many years kept turning up ancient coins. A local rhyme said, 'When the year is turned upside down, then treasure will be found in Money Mound.' This became true in 1961 when children from a school in Crawley excavated, and found Roman coins, fragments of pottery and a burial chamber. If you turn 1961 upside down, then it is still 1961.

R

⁘ RYE ⁘

◌◦ It was all in vain ◌◦

Sadly sometimes those who go to the aid of others end up losing their lives, which is what happened in the case of the *Mary Stanford* lifeboat disaster when the entire crew of seventeen was lost. The story began early on 15 November 1928, when a south-westerly gale with winds gusting over 80mph ravaged the English Channel, leaving many ships in difficulties. At 5 a.m. the maroons were fired, informing the crew of the troubled *Alice of Riga* that help was on its way. The Latvian vessel had collided with a large German cargo ship, *Smyrna*, a little out of Sussex, at Dungeness. The *Alice of Riga* had lost her rudder and was holed and taking in water as she drifted helplessly. Those helping the crew to launch the lifeboat struggled in the wind to get to the lifeboat house a mile or so from Rye harbour. After three attempts the *Mary Stanford*, a non-self-righting fourteen-oar boat, was launched around 6.45 a.m. Five minutes later Rye coastguards received a message that the crew of the *Alice of Riga* had been rescued by the *Smyrna*, and the lifeboat wasn't needed after all. Despite efforts to contact the lifeboat, the crew were too busy coping with the spray and rain to see the recall signal. The mate on the SS *Halton* reported seeing the lifeboat 3 miles from Dungeness and everything appeared to be fine. A little later a young sailor on the *Smyrna* also saw the lifeboat, but then Cecil Marchant, collecting driftwood on Camber sands, saw the vessel capsize, and ran home to tell his parents. Always a storyteller, he received a clout for his efforts but his father thought that perhaps he should report it to the coastguards. Soon rumours spread around the seafaring community. Then at midday the official confirmation came that the *Mary Stanford* was seen bottom up drifting towards land. Over a hundred men rushed to the shore, and every possible effort was made to try to revive fifteen of the crew washed ashore. But it was too late, and two hours later the bodies were taken to Lydd for identification. The national and local papers carried stories of the disaster. Rumours about the lifeboat's demise were rife, and it was wrongly assumed that the lifejackets had become waterlogged and the weight dragged the crew under. The community was devastated, as the crew had grown up and worked together. Eighteen dependent wives and parents and eleven children were left to grieve. Hundreds of people attended the mass funeral held on 20 November, including members of the Latvian Government who felt it was their duty to pay their respects as the lifeboat was going to assist a Latvian vessel. The bodies of two crew members had not been found in time for the funeral, but three months later the body of Henry Cutting came ashore at Eastbourne. Unfortunately the body of the youngest member of the crew, 17-year-old John Head, the coxswain's son, was never found. A court of enquiry sat in December, and in January 1929 they concluded that as there were no survivors the cause of the capsizing was a matter of speculation, but the evidence suggested it was most probably caused by making for the harbour on a strong tide, in dangerous weather conditions. The *Mary Stanford* was eventually taken to the RNLI depot in London where she was dismantled and broken up. The lifeboat house was closed as a mark of respect and never used again. A fine memorial to the men, presented by the people of the Isle of Man and made of Manx stone, can be seen at Rye Harbour. Above the statue of a lifeboatman are the words: 'We have done that which was our duty to do.' A very fitting memorial, I feel.

Memorial to the men who tried to save a ship (Conrad Hughes)

೧೦ *Gobbling turkey* ೧೦

Once upon a time there was a monastery near Turkey Cock Lane, so named because of an interesting story about one of the monks. He was from the Austin Friars monastery on cobbled Conduit Hill, and it is said that he fell in love with a peasant girl living nearby. He watched her every day and became so besotted by her that he attempted to woo her with his beautiful singing voice. Eventually she fell for him, and they decided to run away together. Unfortunately they were spotted, and the monk was put into a cell outside the town walls, which was then bricked up leaving him to die a long lingering death. Devastated, the girl returned to her home, turned her face to the wall, and died of a broken heart. It is said that the ghosts of the couple meet in the lane and her beloved monk still tries to sing to her, but it sounds more like a turkey gobble: the very sounds that he made gasping for air in his bricked-up prison.

೧೦ *If only he had not borrowed that cloak* ೧೦

A great party was to be held on 17 March 1742 on board a ship anchored at Rye harbour. John, the 18-year-old son of the town mayor, James Lamb, was to make his first voyage and the captain had invited the mayor to attend the farewell dinner. With such an important guest to entertain the captain wanted to impress. Soon it was the talk of the town, and rumours spread that French brandy had been smuggled on board and that a lavish extra delicacy of meat was being prepared for the table. On the evening of the dinner, Allen Grebell called in on his brother-in-law the mayor and found him very unwell; in fact he told him he couldn't face the prospect of tucking into such rich food and drink, but he didn't want to let the captain or his son down. The mayor thought for a minute; why not ask Allen to take his place? After all, Allen was a former mayor and he felt sure the captain would be delighted at least to have a mayor present. Allen agreed, saying he would be delighted and was looking forward to the evening, but first he must go home and fetch a cloak. It had been a cold biting day with sleet showers, and he would need something to keep him warm as he made his way to the harbour. 'No need,' said James. 'Take mine, and go and enjoy the evening and make sure you give my apologies to my son.' Thrilled to receive his unexpected invitation, the ex-mayor made his way to the harbour wrapped in the warm mayoral robe. Previously John Breads, butcher and owner of the Flushing Inn, had been heavily fined by James Lamb, then a local magistrate, for selling his meat short in weight. John was known for his sullen way and bad temper, and he would brood over those grievances he could not resolve by fighting, and after a few drinks in his inn he would make vicious jibes to his cronies about butchers not liking lambs. Over time the grievance had grown into an obsession, and Breads vowed that one day he would get his revenge on Lamb. The forthcoming dinner had become a talking point in the inn, and most probably the meat for the dinner had been ordered from Breads, who decided this was the perfect time to get even with Lamb. After closing time he made his way to the parish churchyard and hid behind one of the tombstones. As the parish clock struck a quarter to midnight he pulled his dark cloak around him to keep out some of the cold chilly wind and waited. Soon a solitary none-too-steady figure picked his way through the churchyard, and in the moonlight Breads could see the mayoral red cloak. He grabbed his opportunity, tiptoed from his hiding place and stabbed the man twice deep in the back. Breads casually threw the knife into the undergrowth and made his way home, jubilant, shouting, 'Butchers should kill Lambs', believing he had at last got even with Lamb. Allen must have made the most of the brandy on board because he wasn't aware that he had been stabbed. He staggered the short distance to his home and told his manservant that a drunken man had jostled with him as he crossed the churchyard, and he felt rather shaken. 'You go up to bed,' he told the manservant, 'and I will sit here for a minute in front of the fire, then I'll retire.' Wrapping the mayoral cloak around him he sat down in the parlour to recover. Meanwhile the mayor, feverish from his illness, was drifting in and out of a disturbed sleep dreaming of his late wife, Allen's sister, who appeared to him twice, speaking of her concerns for her brother. Each time he dismissed it and tried to drift back to sleep, but when it happened for the third

Lamb House (Conrad Hughes)

time as dawn was breaking, he decided to get up, dress and cross the road to his brother-in-law's house. He managed to rouse the servant who assured him that his master had returned safely, just after midnight, but the mayor was still uneasy, and asked his servant to go to Allen's bedroom to see if he was all right. White-faced, the servant returned and said his bed was empty and had not been slept in. Together they went to the parlour and found Allen slumped in the chair in front of the dying fire. The mayor shook him gently, but he slumped to the floor having bled to death. The servant was arrested as being the last person to see Allen alive, but in an hour or so he was released. The following day Breads boasted to everyone that 'Butchers kill Lambs', and to make matters worse the knife was discovered in the churchyard, a bone-handled knife with John Breads's name engraved on it. He was arrested and taken to the Ypres Tower, and tethered to the iron ring in the floor. His trial was set for 5 May 1743 and the presiding magistrate was none other than James Lamb, the very man he meant to kill, a unique happening in legal history. Breads, asked what he had to say on the matter, was defiant to the end, and shaking his fists, he shouted, 'I did not mean to kill Mr Grebell. It was you I meant it for and I would murder you now, if I could.' On 8 June, Breads was taken from the Ypres Tower to the Flushing Inn for a last farewell drink with his cronies, and then hanged outside the Strand Gate. The next day Breads's body was cut down and put in an iron cage, and hung from a gibbet on Gibbet Marsh to the west of Rye. Breads's decomposing body remained there for fifty years until only the skull remained as a warning to others. Today it is in the Town Hall.

෨ *Most haunted* ෨

One of the prettiest and most atmospheric streets in the town must be Mermaid Street, once the town's main road, and filled with an assortment of timber-framed houses. The Mermaid Inn is probably the most famous smuggling pub in Sussex, and is where the infamous Hawkhurst Gang would smoke their pipes, loaded pistols on the table, openly boasting about their exploits. The cellars date from 1156 when the original inn was built; it would have been constructed of laths, wattle and daub and plaster, and the innkeeper of the day would have charged one penny a night for lodgings. The black and white timber-framed and tiled building was reconstructed around 1420, retaining its old cellars, and was again renovated in the sixteenth century. But the inn is known most of all for its hauntings, and has been named the most haunted pub in Britain. In all there are thirty-one rooms, spread over several floors, and eight have four-poster beds. Room 1 is said to be haunted by a white or grey lady who sits in the chair by the fireplace. In the morning when guests wake they are puzzled to find that clothes put on this chair overnight are wet, despite no windows being open. In room number 10 resides the ghost of a man whose passion is to walk through the bathroom wall into the main room, frightening many a guest. The Elizabethan room, number 16, was once the scene of a duel between two men, both wearing sixteenth-century clothing. It is said that after fighting their way through rooms, one man finally ended up being killed in this room, before being dragged into another room and thrown down the trapdoor to the cellar below. Room 16 is also haunted by the girlfriend of one of the Hawkhurst Gang who was killed by another member because she knew too much and he was afraid she would expose the men's exploits. Another member of the gang, Thomas Kingsmill, has number 17 named after him. Here the ghost of George Gray's wife, another gang member, haunts a rocking chair, but the chair had to be removed from the premises because it kept disturbing too many guests. An American guest staying in room 19 became so terrified at seeing a man dressed in old-fashioned clothes sitting on his bed, that he spent the rest of the night in an adjacent room with a mattress pulled around his head! In the dining room there is a beautiful seventeenth-century oak chair that is carved to look like a devil. It

Entrance hall to the Mermaid Inn

is said to have once belonged to a witches coven, and is cursed and considered to be very unlucky. The landlady said that a party of schoolchildren came to the Mermaid on a tour to learn about its history, and one little girl misbehaved throughout the entire tour; when they were explaining about the chair, and told the children not to touch it, this little girl immediately jumped up and sat on it. The following day the landlady received a call to say that the child had broken her leg! Was it an unlucky accident or fate? I will leave you to decide.

∾ *Rye's Romeo and Juliet* ∾

Romeo and Juliet had their balcony in Verona, but closer to home Charles and Elizabeth had their own meeting place on the lovers' seat. Elizabeth Boys and Charles Lamb met at a ball in 1785 and fell in love. She was the only daughter of Samuel Boys, a very wealthy landowner and High Sheriff of Kent, who strongly disapproved of the relationship and tried to separate his daughter and Charles, who was then a lieutenant in the Royal Navy. In the hope of breaking the pair up Samuel sent his daughter to live with a relative in Fairlight Place. Unknown to Samuel, Charles had been placed in command of a revenue cutter as part of the anti-smuggling campaign. The *Stag* patrolled along the Sussex coast, and because of his success at catching smugglers he became known as Captain Lamb. However, whilst on leave in Rye he was reunited with his beloved Elizabeth, and whenever his vessel was in the area the two would meet at a secluded spot between Fairlight and Warren Glen, on a sandstone rock that projected out over a stone bench to form a ledge, some 20ft from the beach below. Elizabeth would often go to the spot and look out for her lover in his cutter. Samuel refused the couple permission to marry, and threatened to cut her out of his will if she married her young naval officer. But she was defiant and said she would marry Charles whatever he said. One night Charles brought a boat to the bay below the cliffs, and through the darkness she carefully picked her way down the path to meet him, and they eloped. They were married at St Clement Danes church on the Strand in London on 16 January 1786 and settled in Salehurst. True to his word, when Elizabeth's father died in 1795, he had indeed cut her out of his will and left his large estate to his nephew. The couple had one daughter, Elizabeth Dorothy, born in 1788, and when she married the Rev. Thomas Ferris in 1809, her parents retired to Southampton. The attraction of the sea was always strong and one day in 1814 while cruising around the Southampton waters in his yacht, Charles drowned, leaving Elizabeth a widow after twenty-eight years of marriage. Later his body was washed up near Bognor Regis and he was buried at nearby Thakeham. In later life Elizabeth would travel to Hastings and stay at Marine Parade and visit their secluded spot. She was, no doubt, remembering the happy times together. Sadly the bench at Rye is no more. In 1910, a landslip took a large section of the cliff which was then fenced off, but a further major landslide in 1980 destroyed the famous sandstone crag.

✥ ST LEONARD'S FOREST ✥

∾ *Dragons and a princess* ∾

Most Sussex folk know that St Leonard's Forest, near Horsham, was home to dragons, and where St Leonard, a sixth-century French hermit, once lived. It is said that he fought a long battle with a dragon and eventually won. He was badly wounded and dripping blood, and God made white lilies cover the ground where his blood was spilled. As a reward for freeing the local people from the dragon St Leonard asked God to banish all snakes from the forest, and as the nightingales disturbed his daily prayers he asked that they could be silent, which gave rise to the traditional rhyme:

> *Here the adders never sting,*
> *Nor the nightingales sing.*

Grave of the Black Princess
facing Mecca (Conrad Hughes)

But St Leonard was not the only person to live in the forest. Halima, or Helena Bennett, nicknamed the Black Princess, lived there around 200 years ago. Halima was born in Lucknow, India, in 1772 and was the daughter of a Persian colonel serving in India. At the age of 10 she was betrothed to a local maharajah, Nawab of Pundri, who was 72, but before the marriage could be consummated he died. In 1787, at 15, the young Halima fell in love with a French mercenary soldier, General Benoit De Boigne, and the couple had two children, a son and a daughter, and came to England to live. When De Boigne's father died and he inherited his father's estate and the title of count, he deserted Helena and returned to France to marry a French lady. Helena became a Catholic, and for the last fifty years of her life lived in a cottage at Colgate, a small village at the northern edge of St Leonard's Forest. She died in 1854 at the grand age of 83, and tradition claims she was buried Muslim fashion facing Mecca – north to south and not the usual east to west – at St Mary's churchyard in Horsham. It's a good story, but the more likely explanation is that the churchyard was closed in 1852, and Helena was squeezed into the only available space by the gate.

⁂ SEAFORD ⁂

∾ *A day no one wanted to remember* ∾

The scene that greeted the residents of Seaford on the morning of 7 December 1809 was one of absolute chaos. The tragedy, which became known as the Seven Ships Disaster, happened in the days when privateers attacked and robbed enemy vessels during wartime. Although Napoleon's fleet were defeated, the French were still trying to strangle their enemy by preventing foreign merchant ships from reaching our shores, so ships travelled in convoy. On this particular day the escort ship was the *Harlequin*, leading twenty-two merchant ships through the English Channel as far as Dover. Some had been captured and re-captured, so the crews were aware of the dangers and employed the *Harlequin* to protect the fleet against enemy attack. Like a shepherd it was responsible for making sure none of the flock strayed, but in such stormy conditions it was actually the shepherd that led the flock astray.

The tragic story begins on the afternoon of Tuesday 5 December 1809 when HMS *Harlequin* was escorting a convoy under the command of a young naval officer, Lieutenant Philip Anstruther from Plymouth. On board were four passengers, a couple with a 2-year-old and a baby. At around three o'clock that afternoon the signal for sailing was given and the sails on the respective vessels unfurled. Twenty-three ships left port, and a log entry by the captain shows his frustration with some of the convoy: 'I caused signal guns to be discharged regularly, as handier ships were tending to forge ahead of their allotted station in convoy.' During that night the weather become more turbulent and the shifting winds prevented heavily laden ships from making much headway, but slowly the fleet inched its way along the Channel. By Wednesday evening the convoy met a hurricane, the temperature dropped, and driving sleet and rain made visibility poor, and by the following morning the wind had subsided only to be replaced by thick fog and sleet. The *Harlequin*, as pilot and protector, constantly fired its cannon to indicate her position, but as the day progressed the wind and sleet increased and the fog thickened, so that by 4 p.m. visibility was extremely poor. Lieutenant Anstruther believed the fleet had cleared Beachy Head, and changed course to steer inshore. In his log he wrote: '… estimate Beachy Head now due north. *Harlequin* regains position ahead of convoy. Signal guns fired. Pre-arranged alteration of course to nor'east.' The six leading vessels behind the *Harlequin*, *Unice*, *Albion*, *Weymouth*, *February*, *Traveller* and the *Mitbedacht*, were duty bound to follow their leader, but unfortunately they were not due south of Beachy Head but 3 or 4 miles westwards sailing towards Seaford Bay. The crews had no idea of the danger until they found themselves amongst the violent surf and in due course all seven ships ran aground in the bay. All they could hear above the howling wind was the snapping of masts and the ripping of the sails. Huge breakers from the ebbing tide caused the vessels to crash against each other like toy boats. Captain Anstruther's last log entry reads: '5 minutes to morning watch. Wind sou'west abating. Fog. Sleet. *Harlequin* aground. Signal guns fired and flares to warn convoy. We have serious hull damage from below and mid-ships.' Despite the chaos the crew of the *Harlequin* continued to fire its cannon to warn the rest of the fleet of impending danger. It was thanks to these efforts that the other sixteen merchantmen of the fleet sailed past Beachy Head without further loss of life. In an attempt to ease the strain on the *Harlequin*, the crew were ordered to throw all guns overboard and cut away the masts, but two crew members were killed as they worked on deck and were washed overboard. We can only surmise what it must have been like for the crew trying to move huge guns with the ship rocking in rough seas and the swell washing over the decks. In such appalling conditions the lifeboats could not be lowered, and the *Harlequin* was the first to strike the shore; astonishingly, though, no further lives were lost. Meanwhile, at Seaford Head the barge *Weymouth* came crashing through the shallow waters, breaking up beneath the cliffs. Her cargo of tobacco, cork and barilla (a sodium carbonate and sodium sulphate alkali ash produced by burning various Mediterranean plants, used in the manufacture of soap and glass) bobbed among the waves. Only four of the crew of ten reached shore, and the hero of the rescue was Mr Ginn of Lewes Barrack Department, who at great personal risk led the rescue, managing to drag the four to safety including the cabin boy clutching the master's pet raccoon in his arms. He was determined to save the animal as he was so grateful for the kindness showed to him by the master. The next vessel to come to grief, half a mile west of Seaford Head, was the small brigantine *Traveller*, she was on her way from Malaga with a cargo of dried fruit. Her entire crew of twelve, including master Thomas Coulson, was saved by coming ashore before the ship went to pieces, but her cargo was lost. Not far from the *Traveller* the schooner *Albion* under the command of Captain Jermond lumbered on to the beach, but the ebbing tide caused her to roll on to her side opposite the Martello Tower. The crew of nine lashed themselves to the rigging calling for help, and were eventually saved. Part of her cargo of brandy, saffron, cork, wood and almond had been landed at Plymouth Sound but the remainder was still on board. Just west of the *Harlequin* the American vessel *Unice* ran aground, and Mr Close of Newhaven, together with men from the 81st Regiment rescued the captain and his crew of ten, plus a sizeable part of the cargo of cotton, pearl and potash. The *Midbedacht* was another strong vessel, from the same German company as *February*, and was another of the convoy to flounder with such severe force that the main and mizzen masts and fore-topmast were destroyed when she went aground. Twelve of her crew drowned, only one survived. It was said that the weight of her cargo of brandy, wine, sugar, coffee and other merchandise was responsible for causing her to destruct so quickly. A great deal of the wine was saved, and the local people made good use of the windfall by drinking from anything they could lay their hands on, including hats. Some of the wine-butts floated a considerable distance when the hull broke up, but the customs officers were eventually successful in securing these for the owners. It was the firing of the cannons that morning to warn the fleet of impending danger that woke the inhabitants of Seaford, who then flocked to the long stretch of shingle, unable to do much in the thick fog. As streaks of daylight broke through, the true horror became apparent. Five ships lay near the *Harlequin* at the east end of the bay, and half a mile or so further east was the seventh, the *Weymouth*. The *Sussex Weekly Advertiser* reported, 'They beheld the spectacle that was truly dreadful, the seven ships being high together and complete wrecks, with the remaining crews clinging to differing parts of them, imploring for assistance which is natural in such cases.' Throughout the morning there were numerous rescues and acts of bravery, and by 10 a.m. all that could be saved were ashore; but as with all wrecks the local residents were not averse to a spot of plundering. The *Sussex Weekly Advertiser* reported that it 'found it hard to record the thieving and looting that went on, being ashamed to mention that such dastardly acts could have been committed at a time of such bravery, sorrow and heroism'. Even before the dark of night had lifted, there were men on the beach drunk to oblivion. Two men who had broached brandy cases died either from exposure due to the foul freezing weather or from alcohol poisoning. Even some of the rescuers had their belongings stolen. An officer who had placed his jacket on the beach returned to find his gold watch missing, and Mr Harrison, the Newhaven customs collector, who helped to save three men, lost his overcoat and boots which he had cast off before rushing into the sea to save a sailor.

Whilst some bundled the survivors up the beach to the New Inn (now the Wellington) to be dried, re-clothed and fed, others were busy running back and forth between their homes and the beach with the goods they had stolen, and Captain Browne whilst carrying out a rescue found that looters had stolen his greatcoat. Twelve days later the broken hulls of the ships were auctioned, and on 24 January the insurers auctioned the stores and equipment that had drifted ashore. Bodies from the vessels were washed ashore between 14 and 21 December, and in most cases bodies could not be identified as belonging to an individual ship, so the inscription on the grave reads 'Belonging to one of the above.' Two further bodies were washed up at West Dean and buried there, and almost two months later the body of the last seaman to be recovered was identified as John Callum and buried at Seaford. The following year a court of inquiry was held, and found that no blame should be attached to Lieutenant Anstruther, who was allowed to continue his naval career, as he was faced with appalling weather conditions at a time when none of the modern navigation aids were available to him.

∾ *Never again!* ∾

I expect these were the sentiments expressed by all the children who enjoyed an unexpected windfall of sweeties in 1925. The *Comtesse de Flandre* came to grief in Seaford; thankfully everyone on board was rescued by breeches buoy from the cliff top. The story was well reported in the national press, but the *Comtesse de Flandre* will always be remembered by the children of Seaford as the ship that give them a bellyache. The vessel was carrying a cargo of half-processed liquorice, and whispers soon spread around the classrooms that 'sweeties' had been scattered all along the shore. The children could hardly wait for the school bell to ring signalling the end

An engraving of the
Seven Ships Disaster
(Seaford Museum
and Heritage Society)

of the school day. Then there was a frantic scramble to get out of the school and down to the beach first, with plenty of pushing and shoving. One enterprising boy even 'borrowed' his neighbour's old penny-farthing, but having rushed off he soon realised he had no idea how to stop the machine. In panic he grabbed a conveniently positioned branch of a tree, and hung there as he watched the cycle travel on. Once on the beach, the boys stuffed themselves full of the liquorice, but the next day there was a distinct absence of children, and it was reported that the few who did manage to make it to school spent most of their time queuing in the playground for the outdoor lavatory!

⁂ SELMESTON ⁂

∾ *Mayday, Mayday* ∾

With so many misfortunes happening around the treacherous Sussex coast it seems rather fitting that the inventor of the 'Mayday' distress call, Frederick Stanley Mockford, should be buried in the county. At one time SOS (...---...) was the equivalent to the Mayday call. The Morse code distress call had been adopted by the German Government in 1905. Mockford was born in 1897 and after leaving school he became a Morse code operator for the London, Brighton and South Coast Railway. When the First World War broke out he quickly volunteered for the newly formed Royal Flying Corps, and was sent to France with the first wireless telegraphy unit. Soon he was put in charge of the installation of two-way radio telephones for all aircraft. When the war ended he became an official in the newly formed Air Ministry and helped with the early development of wireless communications for civil aviation, and was the first examiner for candidates applying for their air operator's licence. He then joined Croydon Airport as a senior radio officer and attended many international conferences where aircraft communications were discussed. He invented the code commonly used today by the emergency services, A for Alpha, B for Bravo, C for Charlie etc. Around this time he was asked if he could think of a word that would indicate distress and also be easy to understand by anyone faced with an emergency situation. As so much of the traffic at the time operated between Croydon and Le Bourget Airport in Paris, he suggested the word 'Mayday', from the French *m'aidez*, a shortened version of *Venez m'aider* which means 'come help me'. In 1927, at the International Radiotelegraph Convention of Washington, the voice call Mayday was adopted as the radiotelephone distress call to replace the SOS radiotelegraph (Morse code) call. Three years later Mockford joined the Marconi Company, where he later became the assistant sales manager, then manager of the company's aircraft department, before becoming deputy general manager. In the Second World War he was personal assistant to the chairman, and continued working on war contract

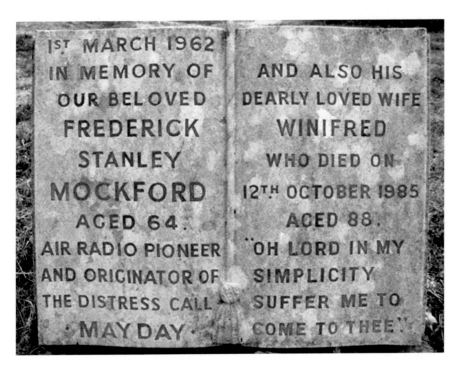

Stanley Mockford's gravestone in Selmeston (Conrad Hughes)

negotiations. Two years after the war ended he was appointed commercial manager, and stayed in this post until his retirement. Sadly Mockford never received an honour from the British government for his work, but he was made a Knight of the Order of the Falcon (an Icelandic award of merit). We will never know how many lives his suggestion saved, but I am sure there are many around the coast of Sussex who will always be grateful to him.

⚜ SHOREHAM ⚜

∾ *A building with a chequered past* ∾

It seems perfect for the oldest secular building in Britain to end up as a museum showing the town's maritime and local history from prehistoric to medieval times, because the building itself must have been part of the fabric of medieval history. Even today Marlipins, a Grade II listed building, does not look too conspicuous among its more modern counterparts, and has sat on the same site, or at least the northern wall has, since 1167 or 1197. It is noticeable because of the Caen stone chessboard pattern on its frontal façade, which is thought to have been added in

Marlipins Museum

the late thirteenth century. The origins and its intended purpose are a mystery, but theories range from a storehouse for wool and hides, a hospital, the remains of the Carmelite Priory, and even a meeting-house for the Knights Templar. It has also been suggested that it was built for ecclesiastical purposes, but no real evidence for this has been found. Like its chequered exterior it seems to have had an eventful past. A look at the deeds for the building which survive from 1347 does not give us a conclusive answer. They describe it as an Oat Market; later it belonged to the Prior of Lewis and became known as his cellar. In 1346 it was sold, and described as a stone corner tenement, but it wasn't until 1703 that the spelling of Marlipins is first recorded. The name Marlipins is also puzzling and is thought to have been derived from a fourteenth-century board game, correctly known as 'merels', a game played between two players each having a set number of pins, pegs, discs or pebbles. The word 'merel' is derived from the word in Old French meaning a token, coin or counter. Local legend tells us it was a Saxon word for tax, although there is no evidence of this, or that the pins referred to a pin of ale, a pin being equal to half a firkin (four and a half imperial gallons or twenty litres), and remembered in the name polypins.

∞ *All for half a sovereign* ∞

Twenty-four year-old James Rook was in jubilant mood when he met his friends at the Red Lion on a cold November evening in 1792. Drink had loosened his tongue, and he was boasting how he and his friend, Edward Howell, had robbed the driver of the local mail, with no need to resort to violence as the driver was relieved of a letter containing a half sovereign, around £50 today and a huge amount in those days. The mail coach was on its usual route from Brighton to Shoreham when, at Goldstone Bottom, near Hove, the two men did the evil deed. Unknown to James, the well-known Brighton female soldier Phoebe Hessel (see Brighton) was enjoying a drink and overheard him. Being an upright citizen she passed on the information to local constable Bartholomew Roberts, and soon the pair were arrested, tried and convicted. On 26 April 1793 a large crowd gathered as the two men were brought to Peterdene Lane accompanied by a military and police escort to be hung in iron frames on a gibbet. Before being strung up Howell asked if the gibbet could be high enough from him to see the Prince's Cricket Ground in Brighton. While the bodies were decomposing James Rook's distraught mother would slip out of her cottage in Old Shoreham and travel to Hove every night, where, under the cover of darkness, she would collect the decaying flesh and bones of her son that had fallen, and placed them in a chest. Eventually she buried them in the graveyard at St Nicholas's church.

The Red Lion at Shoreham (Conrad Hughes)

◌ *Identified by his dog* ◌

Sometime in the 1850s a man broke into Buckingham House with the intention of robbing it, but he was caught in the act by the manservant and, as he tried to make his getaway, he was shot dead by the same manservant. Unfortunately for the thief, no-one knew who he was. It was suggested he be placed in a coffin with a glass lid and displayed in the Red Lion in the hope that someone could identify him. Hundreds of people came to file past the coffin, but eventually it was the man's dog that identified him. One day it somehow got into the inn, and once it saw its master's face it sat by the body and refused to leave. Later the man was identified as John O'Hara and he was buried at St Nicholas's churchyard.

⚜ SLINDON ⚜

◌ *Bowled over* ◌

Slindon is considered to be the home of cricket, but no-one knows where the first cricket match was played, although it seems clear that the game originated in the sheep-grazing counties of southern England, where the short grass of the downland pastures made it possible to bowl a ball of wool or rags at a target. That target was usually the wicket-gate of the sheep pastureland, which was defended with a bat in the form of a shepherd's crooked staff. An ancient mural dating from the fourteenth century in Cocking church, just north of Chichester, depicts shepherds carrying 'cricks', similar to hockey sticks, but heavier and longer. In 1622, complaints were made to the Bishop of Chichester about men in the village of Boxgrove, adjacent to Slindon, playing cricket in the churchyard, breaking the church windows and endangering the well-being of a small girl! Slindon was a very different place then. It was unruly and violent and many, if not most, of its population were actively involved in smuggling, which centred around the Dog and Partridge Inn on the Common. The game of cricket was also very different with no fixed rules, and games were played on any convenient strip of land, either common land or an area lent by the landlord, which had been cropped short by sheep. The ball was bowled underarm along the ground, where it hopped and bobbed about, depending on the evenness of the turf. The wicket comprised two sticks with a third acting as a bail across the top. The 'bat' was curved, not unlike a club, and the batsman was allowed to hit the ball twice, making life hazardous for the fielders. The match was very much like the arrangement of a duel. The opposing teams and the two umpires would confer prior to the game to decide and agree the rules for that particular game. Sides were not necessarily eleven strong and for single wicket games sides could be of three or five players. There were even one-a-side matches. By 1700 the game was being widely played and gradually spreading north, and in the late 1730s Charles Lennox, the 2nd Duke of

Slindon Village sign
(Conrad Hughes)

Richmond, recovering from a badly broken leg, heard that Slindon had men in its team who had a considerable talent for the game. He became patron and sponsor of the Slindon team, and the Common with its clay surface on fast-draining gravel provided an excellent level and fast pitch which allowed for a more accurate game. At the time, the Newland brothers, Richard in particular, were key to the development of the game. Richard was born in 1713 in the village, and two of his brothers, John born in 1717, and Adam in 1719, also played the game, although very little is known of them apart from what appears in match reports.

Richard was the first great left-handed batsman and bowler whose side took on the best in England, including the famous match in 1740 when an all-England team was beaten by 'poore little Slyndon ... in almost one innings'. Richard later went on to play for Sussex, and was arguably the greatest player of his day, although there are some who say that Robin Colchin ('Long Robin') of Bromley was at least his equal. There is no doubt that there was cricket at Slindon a long time prior to 1741. At that time Richard Newland was 28, and it is thought he'd been playing for Slindon for the decade before, since he was 18 years old in 1731. There is no doubt also that some of the Slindon cricketers were actively engaged in the village's other activity, the smuggling trade. Their star bowler, Edward Aburrow senior (senior because he had a son, also Edward Aburrow, who migrated to play cricket for Hambledon in the 1760s) was a known active smuggler who was jailed in 1745 for 'bearing arms whilst landing prohibited goods' and was lucky not to have been hanged or transported. At about the same time Richard and John Newland were accused of assaulting Griffith Hughes in an incident connected with smuggling, but were later discharged. There were, in fact, five Newland brothers, and it is not known if the two youngest ever played for Slindon as no records exist. Interestingly there were also five Newland girls, and one of these, Susan, married Richard Nyren of Eartham; their eldest son Richard (born 1734) was taught how to play the game by his Newland uncles at Slindon, and later went to Hambledon Club and became their captain. In 1744, the 2nd duke created the world's first known cricket scorecard at a match between Slindon and London at the Artillery Ground at Finsbury. Slindon won by fifty-five runs, and Richard Newland was out for a duck in both innings. The original card is now in Chichester Records Office. Slindon's cricketing heritage is honoured today both by the memorial of 'crick', wicket and ball at the junction of Reynolds Lane and Park Lane, and by the players who still oil their bats, don their pads and walk to the crease on that flat and true Slindon Common pitch. Many years ago members of Hambledon Cricket Club stole one of the original Slindon cricket bats and it still hangs above the bar at the Bat and Ball in Hambledon.

❖ STANMER ❖

∞ *Tell it to the bees* ∞

The ancient story of 'telling the bees' about family births, marriages and deaths is well known; it ensured that bees would not fly away or die, and would continue to produce honey for the family. It is also well known that anyone can talk over their problems with bees, and Sussex folk have a greater admiration for the bees than any other insects, believing they were winged messengers of God. There is a recorded incident that happened to a man in Stanmer. He was rather drunk and stumbled into a garden and said to the owner, 'I see you have bees. I must talk to them about my troubles', and proceeded to lay his head on a hive and began talking. Naturally the bees should have been swarming all over him, but instead they kept absolutely still as though listening. The bee keeper was stunned into silence too, but shortly the drunk stood straight and left saying, 'That was good, I feel much better now.' We are also told that during the nineteenth century a woman told her neighbour that her baby daughter had died, because she had forgotten to tell the bees about the birth.

❖ STREAT ❖

∞ *V for Victoria and E for Elizabeth* ∞

The villagers wanted to mark Queen Victoria's Golden Jubilee with something unusual and something that could be seen for miles. What better site than on the curving downs above the village, but what could they erect? Why not the giant letter V, someone must have said. That is exactly what they did, but not just a painted V; they used beech, fir and lime trees arranged in the shape of a V that filled the space from the bottom of the slope to the top. Such a large memento would have required a lot of trees, a very costly project, but as with most ideas it fell upon the local gentry of the day to help carry it through. Mr Lane of Westmeston Place, only a mile away, paid for the trees on the right-hand side, and General Fitzhugh of Streat provided the trees on the left. The workers on Mr Cornwell's Marchant's Farm brought the trees from Cookbridge nursery 10 miles away and planted them, except for one planted on the Streat side. That was put into the ground by young master Cornwell, the 8-year-son of the farmer. It is said they were well rewarded because they flourished, making it an excellent tribute for the queen's special occasion. It has been suggested that the letters VR for Victoria Regina were intended, but the R had to be abandoned as it proved to be too expensive.

❧ TELSCOMBE ❧

∽ *Thanks to Shannon Lass* ∽

Today the picturesque village of Telscombe has a population of less than fifty, and it would appear to be a place time forgot, if it were not for a landowner who made his money from a particular racehorse. Ambrose Gorham was a bookmaker and racehorse trainer who lived at Stud Farm in Telscombe, but his fortunes changed in 1902 when his horse Shannon Lass won the Grand National against all the odds, and Gorham celebrated by restoring Telscombe church. He purchased Telscombe Farm, including the sheep rights or common pasture land. He eventually owned 260 acres of farmland in the locality, including much of the village, with the exception of the manor, which Charles William Neville purchased from James Ambrose Harman in 1924. He employed many of the villagers and was a local benefactor, giving each child a book and a pair of wellington boots at Christmas. He built the Village Club, a hall near the Manor House, for the village as a place of recreation. Ambrose Gorham helped to restore St Laurence church in Telscombe Village and left two murals, which can be seen today. Later he purchased land in the adjoining area to expand his interests and on his death in 1933 bequeathed his property and land for charitable purposes. He also organised car trips to take the villagers to the carnival in Brighton, and whenever he passed, the girls would curtsey and the boys would take their caps off. The village is still centred around Gorham's legacy. Telscombe received its first water supply thanks to him. Up until 1908 the village relied on rainwater, but that year had been a dry summer so Brighton Corporation and Newhaven District Council decided to bring a water supply to the village. It was formally turned on at a ceremony on 24 July 1909.

❧ TIDE MILLS ❧

∽ *The man with the Midas touch* ∽

Tide Mills is no more, but the derelict village is still known by that name although there are no mills, just a few empty foundations that fill with water from the

All that is left of William Catte's empire (Conrad Hughes)

shifting tides. The story of the village starts in 1780 when William Catte, son of a farmer, was born at Buxted. He married at 21 and when he went to pay for a farm for himself in Robertsbridge he found that his mother had sewn banknotes into the lining of his waistcoat. The couple worked hard, rising at 3 a.m. each morning and as he did the threshing, his wife fed the poultry. He had always been interested in the mechanics of flour grinding and after gaining some experience at a mill in Lamberhurst, he went into partnership with one of his cousins who lived at Bishopstone. Together they leased about a mile of wasteland owned by Lord Sheffield, situated between the mill and the sea, and used part of it for cultivation and converted the rest into a reservoir, filled by the tide to give them extra power for the mills. The first crop of oats from the land paid for the cost of reclaiming the land, which enabled them to increase the mills from five pairs of grinding stones to sixteen, producing 15,000 sacks of flour a week, making it the largest in Sussex. William's motto became 'earn a shilling and save a penny'. The mill stood five storeys high and employed around one hundred workers, and William turned out to be a most generous employer. Most of the workers lived in the village and were paid half a crown (about 12½p) a week. The cottages were fitted and well maintained, and it is said that hardly a day passed without at least one artist setting up an easel to record the idyllic village life. The mill was a masterpiece and William was invited to lecture all over Europe and to offer advice to other millers, but these were changing times, and with the repeal of the Corn Laws in 1846 came the importation of cheaper foreign grain in vast quantities, as well as the advent of steam power, both of which contributed to the demise of the mill. To make matters worse a huge storm in 1876 devastated the mill and caused much damage to the buildings, but the loyal workers struggled on until 1884 when the mill closed. Seventeen years later the building was dismantled. William Catte had died in 1853, and his empire had continued after his death; the village he so caringly created and looked after lived on, until finally in 1936 it was condemned, with the last residents forcibly removed in 1939. With the onset of the Second World War part of the area was cleared to provide an area for fire training and to practise street fighting; then tragedy struck. Perhaps it was an order misunderstood, or maybe Intelligence feared an imminent invasion, but the army arrived, giving everyone just an hour to clear the range, then they blasted the whole village and razed it to the ground. Maybe there was a valid reason for the destruction, but the wounds dug deep and a common phrase amongst the elderly was 'It was our people that did it.'

∞ *Grieving George Catte* ∞

William's luck obviously did not rub off on his son George, who took over running the Tide Mill when his father died. Just three years earlier George had married Mary Ann Cooper, the daughter of his father's business partner, but sadly Mary died in April 1856. George was beside himself with grief and decided he would commemorate the many virtues of his young wife by building almshouses. The first stone was laid on 18 March 1857 and an inscription on vellum was placed in a bottle within the wall. It read: 'This building was commenced, and on this day dedicated to charitable purposes, and the first stone laid, in the presence of the Rev John Harrison, Vicar of this parish and the sorrowing Husband, Mother and Friends of the late Mary Ann Catte, by her nephew, Thomas, eldest son of her Brother Thomas Cooper of Norton in this Parish'. When he laid the stone Thomas was just 6 years old, but eighteen months later he too died. He is buried under the box tomb of his aunt at St Andrew's church, Bishopstone. The almshouses were designed to house three single aged people of either sex or two single people and one married couple.

⚜ UDIMORE ⚜

∞ *The village the angels named* ∞

Local legend informs us that when the ancient church of St Mary was going to be built on Brede Level marshes, the villagers could make no progress. Each morning they found the pile of stones assembled the day before had been moved mysteriously uphill to the church's present position. Fed up with having to bring the building material back down the hill to start again, the villagers decided to stay up and watch to see who the enigmatic stone shifters were. Presently, through the darkness they saw a host of angels gliding towards the stones, who then proceeded to pick them up in their arms and carry them uphill, chanting the words 'O'er the mere! O'er the mere!' Eventually the little church was built and the locals settled

Udimore church (Conrad Hughes)

down to worship on the site the angels had chosen. Over time the village became known as 'O'er the Mere' which soon became changed to Uddimere, and then finally to Udimore. It is claimed that the inhabitants can look forward to a long life, and maybe this has something to do with the angels. 'Widow Marshall, late of this parish' died in 1798 at the grand age of 98, not bad at a time when around 25 per cent of the population died before they were 5 years old and life expectancy was about 40.

Wild service trees, related to the rowan and a remnant of ancient woodlands, are a bit of a rarity these days, but there's one of the biggest, 55ft high with a twisted trunk, near Parsonage Farm. It can't be missed with its distinctive spring May-like blossom or its autumn orange-red leaves. The fruits, regarded as a delicacy, are also known as chequers, and were once used as love potions or made into an alcoholic drink. The origin of the name chequers in unknown, but as there are numerous Chequers Inns in Sussex it is thought the name could come from the name of the fruit used in this favourite tipple.

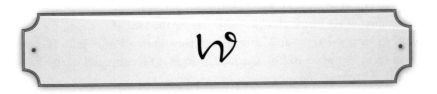

✤ WORTHING ✤

∞ *Worthing's secret ceiling* ∞

Most people who visit another country don't return with such an ambitious an idea as Gary Bevans. You may think the Sistine Chapel ceiling, painted in the sixteenth century by Michelangelo Buonarroti, is unique to Rome, but there is actually a second in our very own county. In the English Martyrs Church in Worthing, there's a most impressive reproduction to rival the one in Rome. It all began in 1987 after a parish pilgrimage trip to Rome to attend the beatification of eighty-five English martyrs, and is the brainchild of Gary Bevans, a sign-writer,

Worthing's own Sistine Chapel ceiling (Conrad Hughes)

parishioner and deacon of the church, a natural artist with no formal training. The artist noted that the Sistine Chapel ceiling was practically the same shape and size as the ceiling of his parish church, and discussed the idea of bringing the 'Sistine ceiling' to his home town at Worthing with parish priest Father John Haughton, who in turn, consulted Bishop Cormac Murphy-O'Connor, who later became Cardinal of England, and permission was granted.

The ceiling is two-thirds the scale of the original and is truly a labour of love, and was solely funded on donations from firms like ICI, a local solicitor and generous visitors. Blank plywood panels were screwed to the ceiling, and working often through the night in summer heats and bitterly cold winters, it took Gary over five years to complete the only known replica outside Rome. It was completed in 1993, and after the Mass of Thanksgiving, attended by many local dignitaries, including the Duke of Norfolk and Countess of Arundel, Gary was presented by the bishop with the papal cross *Pro Ecclesia et Pontifice*. Thirteen national and international TV companies have filmed the ceiling, including CBS, ABC, BBC, ITV, Australian, and New Zealand broadcasters, the most recent being Nippon Television International. Today due to modern developments in sign-writing Gary makes his living by decorating and restoring houses whilst his masterpiece at the English Martyrs Church will live on, featuring in the television programme *Flog It*, as well as receiving an award for excellence in 2014 and 2015 from TripAdvisor.

∞ *A memorial to pigeons* ∞

Another unique Worthing feature sits in the formal gardens at Beach House Park. This is the war memorial to homing pigeons that did the dangerous work of carrying vital military messages. Thirty-two pigeons went on to be awarded the Dickin Medal, recognised as the animal's equivalent to the Victoria Cross, and named after the founder of the PDSA Maria Dickin. It is the only memorial to warrior birds in Britain, and is the creation of local actress and playwright Nancy Price who, together with members of the People's Theatre in London, commissioned the memorial. It was designed by local sculptor Leslie Sharp, who started work on the memorial in 1949, and it was unveiled on 27 July 1951 by the Duke and Duchess of Hamilton. It consists of a circular mound, planted with shrubs, and a rockery with streams and pools of water, two boulders with carved wording, and once had two stone pigeons. The pigeon sculptures were sadly stolen and a fence has been erected around the mound to prevent further vandalism. The stones for the memorial were quarried in the Forest of Dean, and in 1999 were refurbished and repainted.

Boat porches that are unique to Worthing (Conrad Hughes)

∾ *Unique boat porches* ∾

With so many seafaring communities around Sussex it is a mystery why boat porches or arches should be a feature only seen in Worthing. The style, known as 'ogee', has a gentle equally proportioned arch that suddenly peaks at the apex, and originated in the days when fishermen used their upturned boats as shelters to protect their doorways in bad weather. Some of the houses date from 1817–1820, and use the stuccoed porch, which consists of wall plaster and used is on classical mouldings with a decorative double curve as the roof. This is to resemble the bottom of the boat and may have been built by the local fishermen themselves, using their boats as the basis for the design. Fine examples can be seen in Alfred Place, Portland Road and Warwick Place and as there are so few we can assume that the builder either died or moved away.

∾ *Looking out to sea* ∾

One of the most iconic buildings and the oldest working cinema in Sussex must be the Dome Cinema at Worthing. The building was opened in 1911 by

Swiss entrepreneur, actor and theatre manager Carl A. Seebold, who moved to Worthing in 1904. He acquired the site in 1906 and construction began in 1910. It was originally called the Kursaal, a German word meaning 'cure hall', and offered a health centre and entertainment under one roof. It was one of the first multi-entertainment centres in the country, offering roller-skating exhibitions and events in the Coronation Hall and the first cinema in West Sussex at the Electric Theatre, showing short silent cartoons. During the First World War, seeing the number of casualties mounting, the residents in the town objected to the name, and in order to save his successful business, Seebold held a competition for a new name with a prize of £1. It was renamed the Dome, and four residents shared the prize. In 1921 the temporary ranked floor in the Coronation Hall was made permanent and the Dome remodelled, opening in 1922 with *Pollyanna*, starring Mary Pickford. At the same time the Electric Theatre was converted into a ballroom. In 1970 Worthing Borough Council took over the building with the aim of demolishing it to build a shopping complex, but the 'Save the Dome' group rescued it, and it has now been taken over by the Worthing Dome and Regeneration Trust, and is a listed building. It closed in 2005 to undergo a £2.5 million refurbishment, made possible by one of the largest grants awarded in Sussex from the Heritage Lottery Fund, £1.654 million, with English Heritage contributing £250,000. Today besides the regular film programme there is a monthly Monday Club performance for teenagers and adults with special needs,

The Kursaal being built (West Sussex Library Service)

The Dome today (Conrad Hughes)

a Silver Screen performance on the last Wednesday of the month with a mix of classic and modern films, and a Saturday morning children's film performance.

∾ *Worthing's happy bunch of eccentrics* ∾

Every town or village has its eccentric characters, although today you are more likely to see a regular sprinkling of resident tramps and down-and-outs. The eccentrics of yesteryear were exuberant, colourful and harmless, and went a long way to brighten up the day. In front of St Paul's church in Chapel Street, Bubbles, or William Robert Ames, became a well-known town character making thousands of friends as he collected for charity. No-one was quite sure how he acquired his nickname, but some say it was earned as a boy. Before the First World War he worked on the estate of the late King Edward VII, before joining the Norfolk Regiment. He was wounded, not once but three times; in 1915 at the Battle of Mons he received a bullet in his side and was invalided home. He recovered enough to return to the front, but in September that year was hit in the head by a bullet at Loos. Once again he came home to convalesce before returning, but this time he wasn't so lucky when he was wounded in the spine. He spent two years in a hospital bed on his back, before being able to sit in a spinal chair. He started a new life in Gifford House (Queen Alexandra Hospital Home) in 1932 and died following an operation at the age of aged 75. Horace Duke, 'The Duke', or Burlington Bertie as he was known, was a familiar sight, standing at roundabouts, directing the traffic. I suppose today we would call it 'performance art', but Bertie became an excellent ambassador for the town, although he did not confine his activities to Worthing alone, but could be seen at roundabouts at Broadwater, Offington and Shoreham High Street as well as at the entrance to Shoreham beach. He was always elegantly dressed, inspired by his visits to the Brighton Hippodrome and the dress of Max Miller, and rode around on a 'sit up and beg' bicycle or a vintage motorbike. He was always upright and well-mannered, dressed in topper, bowler or boater and plus-four tweeds, or a striped blazer and grey flannel trousers, pristine white gloves, and wearing a monocle, much to the amusement of passers-by. A delivery man recalls a man taking in parcels at Marylebone Optical, dressed in a brown warehouse coat. One day he asked the delivery man if he'd seen the well-dressed man at Offington roundabout, and when he said yes, the man started to show him a large number of photographs of Bertie and went on to say he himself was Bertie, that when he was dressed up he became a completely different person. Bertie loved clothes and would pay high prices for what he wanted on his frequent trips to London, but he warned the delivery man never to acknowledge or talk to him when he was dressed up. Another resident recalls him singing Onward Christian Soldiers as he drove around. Bertie also enjoyed a pint and would often take his drink outside and wave to any passers-by. When he died his coffin, in a glass-sided hearse, was pulled by two black horses.

During the 1950s in Worthing there were any number of eccentric old ladies as well, and a little group of them used to sit in old-fashioned wickerwork bath chairs at Splash Point and watch the waves. For some reason they all had Pekinese dogs which sat in wickerwork shopping baskets on their knees.

∽ *Saved for future generations* ∽

On 17 December 1944 a 49 Squadron Lancaster took off from RAF Fulbeck, loaded with 90,000 tons of bombs and incendiaries destined for Munich. It encountered mechanical problems and lost a great deal of height, and at such a low altitude it would have been impossible to ditch the bombs without causing an explosion destroying the plane. Realising they were over the town of Worthing and seeing the tide was out, they turned seaward. The 24-year-old pilot, Flight Officer Edward Gordon Essenhigh, knowing he would only get once chance, attempted to land on the beach wheels up. Just off Heene Terrace the plane hit a wartime defence and exploded, sending flames high into the sky as well as shrapnel and pebbles. Sadly all seven crew were killed, and as the Lancaster burned, little could be done to save the lone figure of Sergeant Gordon Frederick Callon (rear gunner) aged 20, who could be seen in the gun turret. Finally his body was recovered and buried at

The pilot, Edward Essenhigh,

BACK ROW
E. REES. A. THOMPSON. S. CALLON. J. MOORE   FRONT ROW
L. BOURNE. H. VAREY

Pilot Essenhigh and his crew (www.bombercommand.com)

Littlehampton. The crew are remembered locally in street names; Flight Officer Edward Gordon Essenhigh aged 24, pilot (Essenhigh Drive), Sergeant Gordon Frederick Callon, aged 20 , rear gunner (Callon Close), Harry Varney, aged 24, flight engineer (Varney Road), Sergeant Leonard Bertie Bourne, aged 28, navigator (Bourne Close), Sergeant Frederick Bernard Rees aged 22, wireless operator (Rees Close), Sergeant James Worral Moore, aged 39, mid upper gunner (Moore Close), and Officer James Andrew Thomson, aged 25, bomb aimer, (Thomson Close). There is also a Fulbeck Avenue and a Squadron Drive, named after the squadron, and all the roads are designed to spur off each other.

Essenhigh Drive (Conrad Hughes)

✣ YAPTON ✣

⧙ Close that door ⧚

This village is known as the village that never closes its doors because, some say, Yapton once had a calf which got its head stuck between the bars of a gate, and in order to free it, the distraught farmer had to cut its head off. From then on he decided he would keep all gates and doors open. Another explanation is that to avoid window tax, a man bricked up most of his windows, making the house very dark, so he ordered his servants to leave as many doors open as possible to let light into the house. However, a third tale informs us the doors were left open so a dog could pass through, and not worry the neighbours by its howling when it wanted to go indoors But the one I favour most dates back to the smuggling days, when the local people allegedly left the doors open so that, if chased, the smugglers landing their goods at Climping Beach could find refuge from the King's Men in any house in the village. Rumour claims there is a hidden tunnel in the parish church that was used by smugglers. The vicar once gave a sermon on the evils of smuggling without knowing that beneath his feet was a stash of contraband goods. It is even said that, like many churchyards in Sussex, some of the large tombs were unoccupied, their purpose being to store the booty. One of the villagers was the victim of a horrific murder in 1748. The smugglers had stored some tea in a barn, and when they came to distribute it, they thought they were missing a bag of tea. They suspected three people, John Cockrel and his son who kept an inn in Yapton, or Richard Hawkins who they knew had been working in the barn threshing corn. Arriving at the inn they asked for some ale, then accused the Cockrels of stealing the tea. After severely beating them both they set off in search of Richard, arriving at his house armed with a hatchet. They threatened his wife that if she didn't confess to receiving the tea they would cut off the head of their six-month-old baby. She said she knew nothing and pleaded with the men, so Jeremiah Curtis, John Mills, known as Smoker, and another called Robb set off to find Richard and took him forcibly to a back room at the Dog and Partridge on Slindon Common. These men were all well-known smugglers and Richard said he had no knowledge of the missing tea. Curtis became very annoyed and ranted, 'Damn you; you do know, and if you do not confess I will whip you till you do; for, damn you, I have whipped many a rogue and washed my hands in his blood.' James Reynolds, the innkeeper, was very concerned because these smugglers had a reputation for being ruthless, so he begged Richard, 'Dick, you had better confess; it will be better for you.' But Richard was adamant he had not taken the tea. Reynolds was then ordered to leave the room and Mills and Robb set about beating and kicking Richard. The attack was so ferocious that in his agony he cried out that the Cockrels were involved. Curtis and Mills rushed out taking their horses, and said they would go and fetch them. Meanwhile, at the Dog and Partridge, Robb and another man sat the terribly injured man in a chair by the fire, but he died of his injuries. The two left Richard and rode towards Yapton, meeting Curtis and Mills on the way with the Cockrels following behind. In whispered tones Mills was told that Richard was dead. 'By God!' exclaimed Curtis, 'we'll go through it now,' and Curtis sent the two Cockrels home. The gang rode back to the Dog and Partridge, where Reynolds was in despair, saying, 'You have ruined me.' To which they replied they would make amends. The smugglers thought about how they would dispose of the body; the first option was to bury the body near the inn and say that they had deported Richard to France for stealing their tea. Reynolds objected strongly to having the body so close and said it would be found and he would be implicated. In the end, they laid Richard across a horse and took him to Parham Park, 12 miles away, where they tied large stones to his body, and threw it into the pond. In due course the murder was discovered and the authorities, anxious to bring the smugglers to justice, offered a pardon for information to anyone not involved in murder. Another smuggler, William Pring, had heard gossip about the murder, and wishing to make a new life for himself he decided the gang's fate. They were eventually caught and Mills was found guilty and sentenced to death. He was hanged, then taken in chains to Slindon Common and strung up on a gibbet, near the Dog and Partridge.

∽ *What price for the wife?* ∽

A strange bargain was done at the Shoulder of Mutton and Cucumbers pub when the local rat-catcher by the name of Mr White was lodging at the pub in 1898. White had taken a fancy to the wife of Mr Marley, a roof thatcher in the village, and one night at the bar they decided to do a deal. The rat-catcher could have Mrs Marley, his four children and his furniture, the thatcher being content with 7s 6d (around £40) and a quart of beer! The odd name for the pub seems to come from the tradition of eating cucumbers with lamb, but sadly this historic pub closed down in 2009 and is now two houses.

Old engraving
of Richard
Hawkins beating
at the Dog and
Partridge

∾ *The Black Widow* ∾

And finally to end our tour around this remarkable county, a tale of a copycat
Black Widow murder, which must have shocked the residents of this quiet village.
When the paramedics answered a call from Mrs Thompson in June 1994 she
calmly handed over empty bottles that had once contained aspirin and an antidepressant called Dothiepin, saying she had found her husband dead in bed. Earlier
that evening, she had made her husband an extra spicy curry for his thirty-first
birthday and laced it with the bitter-tasting antidepressant, and plied him with
drinks containing ground aspirin. No-one suspected he had been murdered and
he was buried in the family plot. The crime remained undetected for seven years
and only came to light when Thompson was found not guilty of attempting to
murder her third husband in 2000. She had married Mr Webb bigamously in 1991
while still married to her first husband, Mr Wyatt, against whom she had made false
accusations;, she was forced to go on the run as she had set him up to take the
blame. After killing Mr Webb and eventually divorcing Mr Wyatt she married for
the third time, but they were later divorced after she attacked him with a baseball
bat and a knife, because she said she feared for her life. It is thought she may
have killed Mr Webb to try to incriminate him in a fraud scam at the Woolwich
Building Society where she worked; or perhaps she thought she would benefit

from his death, but his £36,000 death benefit was eventually paid to his mother after she proved they were not legally married, and the money went to charity. It came to light that Thompson had been jailed twice in the past for stealing money from her employers and conning men out of money. Mr Webb's body was finally exhumed in 2001 after a witness told of the spicy curry meal. New tests revealed a much higher level of drugs in the body than first thought, and Thompson was found guilty by a 10–1 majority. The court was told that Mr Webb was a happy fitness fanatic who rarely took medication, but during the last week of his life he was not seen, and Thompson repeatedly told telephone callers that he was ill or depressed. She was ordered to serve fifteen years and 357 days from the date of sentence before she would be considered for parole. The judge said, 'Whether she is then released will be for the parole board to decide, and at that stage they will need to consider the need for the public to be protected from Thompson.' She had committed a 'cold and calculated' murder through trickery and without remorse. One newspaper reported that, 'The men of Britain can sleep safe tonight knowing she has been taken off the streets.'

About the Author

Wendy Hughes turned to writing in 1989 after being diagnosed with a genetic connective tissue disorder called Stickler Syndrome, and has spent many years campaigning and writing on behalf of people affected by the condition. She has written twenty-seven non-fiction books, many on local history, including *Haunted Worthing*, *Shipwrecks of Sussex*, and *Not a Guide to Worthing* for The History Press. She was born on the Gower Peninsula in South Wales and now enjoys living near the sea in Rustington, West Sussex.